MINNESOTA
TERRITORY

WISCONSIN
1848

MICHIGAN
1837

IOWA
1846

NATIONAL ROAD

ARKANSAS
1836

FLORIDA 1845

THE LIFE HISTORY OF THE UNITED STATES

Volume 4: 1829-1849

THE SWEEP WESTWARD

THE LIFE HISTORY OF THE UNITED STATES

Consulting Editor, Henry F. Graff

Volume 4: 1829-1849

THE SWEEP WESTWARD

by Margaret L. Coit

and the Editors of LIFE

A STONEHENGE BOOK

TIME INCORPORATED, NEW YORK

THE AUTHOR of Volumes 3 and 4 in this series, Margaret L. Coit, combines in her work a continuing study of American history and English, both of which she teaches at Fairleigh Dickinson University in New Jersey. This felicitous pairing of interests is seen in her book *John C. Calhoun*, which won many literary honors, including the 1951 Pulitzer Prize for biography. Her other works include a biography, *Mr. Baruch*, and a history, *The Fight for Union*. Born in Connecticut, Professor Coit earned her B.A. at the University of North Carolina, which later awarded her an honorary doctorate.

THE CONSULTING EDITOR for this series, Henry F. Graff, is Chairman of the Department of History at Columbia University.

TIME INC. BOOK DIVISION

EDITOR *Norman P. Ross*
COPY DIRECTOR *William Jay Gold*   ART DIRECTOR *Edward A. Hamilton*
CHIEF OF RESEARCH *Beatrice T. Dobie*

Editorial staff for Volume 4, THE LIFE HISTORY OF THE UNITED STATES

SERIES EDITOR *Sam Welles*
ASSISTANT EDITOR *Jerry Korn*
DESIGNER *Douglas R. Steinbauer*
STAFF WRITERS *Gerald Simons, John Stanton, Harvey Loomis*
CHIEF RESEARCHER *Clara E. Nicolai*
RESEARCHERS *Sheila Osmundsen, Natalia Zunino, Malabar Brodeur, Evelyn Hauptman, Patricia Tolles, Barbara Moir, Barbara J. Bennett, Madeleine Richards, Joan Scafarello*
PICTURE RESEARCHERS *Margaret K. Goldsmith, Theo Pascal*
ART ASSOCIATE *Robert L. Young*
ART ASSISTANTS *James D. Smith, John M. Woods, Douglas B. Graham*
COPY STAFF *Marian Gordon Goldman, Rosalind Stubenberg, Dolores A. Littles*

PUBLISHER *Jerome S. Hardy*
GENERAL MANAGER *John A. Watters*

LIFE MAGAZINE

EDITOR *Edward K. Thompson*   MANAGING EDITOR *George P. Hunt*   PUBLISHER *C. D. Jackson*

Valuable assistance in the preparation of this volume was given by Roger Butterfield, who was picture consultant; Doris O'Neil, Chief of the LIFE Picture Library; Donald Bermingham of the TIME-LIFE News Service; and Content Peckham, Chief of the Time Inc. Bureau of Editorial Reference.

THE COVER, a detail from the picture on pages 146-147, shows a California miner swirling water, pay dirt and dreams in a pan. His presence there represented a dream come true: America one nation from coast to coast.

CONTENTS

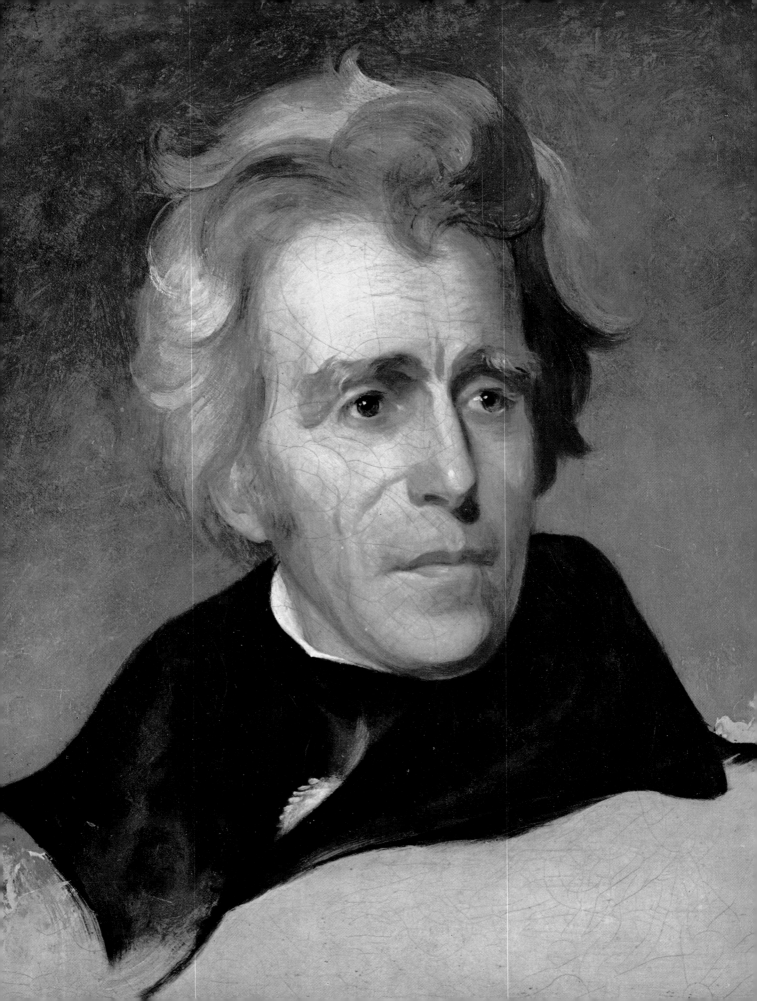

1. THE PEOPLE IN POWER

IN 1796, seven years after President-elect George Washington moved north to his inauguration, a lanky, big-nosed man with reddish hair rode into Philadelphia. He wore not the breeches and buckles of fashion but the rough clothing of the West, and his hair hung in a queue down his back, tied with the skin of an eel, frontier-style. This was the youthful Andrew Jackson, a self-made man with a Western faith in the capacity of the individual. In his view any upstanding citizen who could command men or make a good stump speech had as much right to public office as the rich and well-educated. He himself, the son of a poor Scotch-Irish farmer who lay in an unmarked grave, had already been lawyer, planter, territorial official, soldier and merchant, and now, still not 30, he was his state's first congressman.

Thirty-three years later, Andrew Jackson made another momentous trip to the seat of the government. This time he was President-elect of the United States, the first from the Western part of the nation. Now the whole country knew him—a man with a fiery temper and an ardent sense of justice, both deeply loved and fiercely hated. Former President John Quincy Adams disdained the ceremony at Harvard when Jackson received an honorary degree. Adams refused to attend because he did not want to witness his alma mater's disgrace in conferring her highest honor "upon a barbarian and savage who could scarcely spell his own name."

The presidency did for Jackson what it has often done for the man who

A POPULAR PRESIDENT, the tough but ailing Andrew Jackson is marked by deep lines of suffering even in this rather glamorized portrait by the noted painter Thomas Sully.

Jackson, a controversial President, was threatened with assassination 100 times before a demented Englishman (right) tried it. This was the first presidential assassination attempt in American history. Jackson later insisted his assailant was the tool of his foes—while the foes countercharged that the affair had been staged by the Jacksonians to win public sympathy.

attains its loneliness: his grasp of the office grew almost visibly from the day of his inauguration. In part this was because he was less concerned about himself than any President since Washington. His country was all he had left —life itself now meant very little to him. He was 62 and widowed, and physically he was a wreck, suffering from a hacking cough (he ultimately died of tuberculosis) and severe headaches.

Yet he could be as gentle as a woman, rousing himself from sleep at the faintest sound of a child's cry. During his Administration a number of children —particularly those of his nephew Andrew Jackson Donelson and his adopted son Andrew Jr.—stayed at the White House for periods varying from a few days to several years. At least once, during a measles epidemic, it was the President of the United States himself who picked up a restless little one and walked the floor with him until he slept. But his lantern jaw remained as firm, his mouth as resolute, his blue eyes as piercing as in youth. His rages were legendary, but—at least in his presidency—he used the legend in order to terrorize bullies or self-seekers. A furious outburst of language would swiftly end an unpleasant interview. "They thought I was mad," he would drawl calmly afterward and light up his pipe.

A faith in democracy and a hatred of special privilege burned in him. He was sure, as Jefferson had been, that America was never meant to "become a government of brokers." Unlike Jefferson, he had to cope with this very development. The countryside was seeing the smoke of new industries; the city mobs Jefferson had feared were demanding proof of the democratic faith precisely as were the landholder and the frontiersman.

If huge profits were to be made, Jackson felt, they must be shared with the many; if business had gained great power, then government must also have great power to counter it. His aim would be to fit the Jeffersonian faith to the Jacksonian facts, using the Hamiltonian methods of big government. Jackson's most famous appointee to the Supreme Court, Chief Justice Roger Taney, who was named in 1835, put it this way: "The object and end of all government is to promote the happiness and prosperity of the community . . . and it can never be assumed, that the government intended to diminish its power of accomplishing the end for which it was created."

Jackson's West felt no need to rationalize its resentment of the privileged. A suspicion of the rich was the normal frontier credo and Jackson's beliefs were a natural outgrowth of this attitude. Part of this credo was that anybody could do anything. This is the great dividing line between Jacksonian and Jeffersonian democracy, and it helps explain why, if one judges his impact on American thinking and feeling, Andrew Jackson may well have been the most significant President.

THE story of young America is a kind of Greek tragedy, with the hero flawed in his central being. First, the United States was a nation conceived in liberty yet partly based on an economic foundation of human slavery. This was its original sin, from which it had to be purged. Second, here was a people still living in a dream—Jefferson's dream of a pastoral, independent America that in some miraculous way could escape the penalty of man's innate greed and all the complications of the Industrial Revolution. In that lay the dramatic conflict: a free people striving to make the dream of freedom real and striving to adapt that dream to the challenges which had thwarted freedom elsewhere. From Jackson's time on, the story of the United States is the story of this groping toward reality.

Although Jefferson was a greater man, Jackson was a greater President. Not only did Jackson demonstrate as never before the powers of the presidential office and the force of executive authority to put down challenges and uprisings; during his era (which must include the presidency of his close associate Martin Van Buren) the foundations were laid for the modern two-party system. More important, the Jeffersonian concept of equal rights for all and of the natural aristocracy was thoroughly revised. The intent was no longer to train and seek out the natural leadership, but to demonstrate that all men are literally equal and are potential leaders.

Unlike Jefferson, who believed only in equal opportunity under a trained elite, Jackson believed in the basic equality of all white men. During his administration, democracy was to spread rapidly in the United States. With the extension of the franchise, more than four times as many men would vote in 1836 as in 1824. In every state but South Carolina, presidential electors were now picked by popular vote instead of by the legislatures, and they were expected to vote for the popular choice.

THE first national nominating conventions were held for the election of 1832. These were no unmixed blessing. Just when the choice of a President was being handed over to the voters, the choice of a candidate was taken away from the leaders and handed over largely to the party hacks. The first seven Presidents governed for the people, but were not governed by them. This was not always true thereafter.

The change in political methods was quickly felt at the lowest levels of government. In 1832 the acute French visitor Alexis de Tocqueville, discussing with a Philadelphian the possibility that much of the nation's crime was caused by excessive consumption of liquor, asked a logical question: why, then, was not the tax on alcohol restored? The answer was flat: any official who voted for such legislation would be defeated.

The use of patronage for party purposes was as old as the republic: Jackson helped to establish it in national politics. "To the victor belong the spoils," cynically explained Senator William L. Marcy of New York, and coined a lasting phrase. Actually, however, Jackson did not abuse political patronage under the "spoils system" nearly as much as is widely believed. Estimates of the number of officeholders replaced for party reasons during his eight years in the White House vary between one in five and one in 10, and many of these were discharged for justifiable cause.

The spoils system is important more because it summed up Jackson's philosophy than because of its political effect at the time. That philosophy was not necessarily the same as Marcy's. Jackson felt that no one man had a greater right to public office than the next man—and that no injury was done to the displaced worker since he retained his personal qualities and his basic ability to earn a living. Unfortunately, many of those removed were incapable of making a living elsewhere. Jackson's mistake was in thinking that because he, an ordinary man, could rise to the presidency, any one else could do so. He failed to realize that he was the personification of Jefferson's natural aristocrat.

The difference between Jacksonian and Jeffersonian democracy could be

A lampoon of the Masons pokes fun at their secret signs. They came under attack after William Morgan of Batavia, New York, vanished while writing a book on Masonic secrets. An anti-Masonic party arose against the members of this and other secret groups (including Phi Beta Kappa). But the common man's champion, Jackson, remained proudly a Mason.

traced largely to the difference in the character of the country. Jackson's America had resemblances to modern America: a nation of crowding, change and slums; of crime, poverty and juvenile delinquency; of strikes, riots and mob violence. Although lawbreakers were still lashed and in Boston in 1831 more than 1,500 people were in jail for debt (some owing less than $20), modern industrial America was born in the time of Jackson.

More steamboats were moving on America's waters. Canals were connecting river to river. Little steam cars were running from Lancaster to Philadelphia. The building of the Baltimore and Ohio and the Mohawk and Hudson railroads went on, despite dire warnings of dreadful calamities to livestock near the right-of-way.

It was a period of whooping religious revivals, but the real religion, as outside observers were quick to note, was free enterprise. Already America was "one gigantic workshop," wrote a German visitor. "Business is the very soul of an American." The two greatest changes between 1830 and 1850 were the industrialization of the North and the filling up of the West.

Over two million new Americans from overseas were added to the population in 25 years. The cry was out for help in lumbering the forests, building bridges and cutting canals. The immigrants came in hordes. Ten thousand arrived in 1825, some 23,500 in 1830 and 300,000 in 1849.

Ireland, poor and overcrowded, was virtually emptying itself into the United States. Nearly half of the new arrivals to the United States in 1817 were unskilled Irish. In Philadelphia the Society of United Irishmen was organized to help find employment or a way west for the newcomers. Help was sorely needed. For although the market for unskilled labor west of the Alleghenies was large and growing, most of those arriving—like so many who came later—preferred to huddle in the coastal cities. By the depression year of 1837, city streets were filled with wandering crowds of bewildered aliens.

Bigotry tainted the American atmosphere. White laborers in Philadelphia, thrown out of work by the competition of Negroes, stormed the Negro section of the city and destroyed a church and 30 houses. In Somerville, Massachusetts, an anti-Catholic mob burned a convent in 1834; the charred ruins stood for 35 years as a monument to prejudice. (But at a public meeting in Faneuil Hall, Boston, Protestants united to protect their "Catholic brethren.")

Unschooled, uncontrolled youngsters loitered in the streets, assaulting and insulting passersby, stealing, wrecking, setting fires. One solution might have been to send them to school. But public schools were still rare, and legislation in some states to establish free education had proved ineffective. It would be several years yet before Horace Mann in Massachusetts would rally the Calvinists and Unitarians, the more intelligent workmen, and humanitarians in general to battle for tax-supported schools.

A FEW halting steps were taken in the early 1800s to help the unfortunate, the weak and the unemployed. In Philadelphia a committee attempted to learn who made up the poorer groups, what caused their poverty, and how liquor and loan sharks contributed to their misery. In New Hampshire tavern owners were supplied with lists of chronic alcoholics and were fined if they served them. Philadelphia also made a survey to determine how many of the poor would move west to find work. There were plenty of jobs for those who would go. The newcomers fared best in the rural areas. "This be a main

A fashionable couple whirls in a daring new dance, the waltz. A great rage in Paris in 1795, the dance crossed the Atlantic early in the 19th Century. In America it shocked those pious folk who still considered dancing immoral. But it was widely taught by foreign dancing masters, soon became acceptable and was replaced as the scandalous vogue by the polka.

queer country," observed a Yorkshireman on learning that laborers sometimes ate four meals a day; he had had two scanty ones at home.

The cities were another story. In 1831 in the mills of Massachusetts 15,000 women made shoes for 60 cents a week. In Boston it was said that the average Irishman had a life expectancy of only 14 years after reaching the city. In Fall River an employer said that he would use up his factory hands until they were worn out, then discard them like broken machines.

In Jackson's time, labor began to assert itself as a political force to be reckoned with. A national trades union was formed, and there was agitation for a 10-hour workday. In one city 21 labor societies, with 4,000 members, marched on parade, and the fiery journalist William Leggett denounced the courts for using the conspiracy laws against strikers.

As the North became more industrialized a growing uneasiness developed in the agricultural South. In 1828, the year before Jackson took office, Congress had passed a tariff for the declared purpose of protecting northern manufacturers and businessmen. Many Southerners were profoundly convinced that the factory system of the North spelled the doom of their agrarian economy, and to some of these men this "Tariff of Abominations" seemed to be the last straw.

Prominent among the tariff's adversaries was the Democratic vice-presidential candidate. All during the long days of that summer, John C. Calhoun moved like a restless shadow back and forth, back and forth between the white columns of his South Carolina house, Fort Hill, trying to work out a Southern solution to the oppressive tariff. The result of his thinking would pose one of the towering dilemmas of the Jackson Administration—and would mark the course of Southern history from that year to Appomattox.

Calhoun did not fully comprehend the long-range economic trends. During the late 1820s, it is true that Massachusetts was prospering and South Carolina was sinking into poverty. But South Carolina, with its undiversified agriculture, was not the whole South. So far as the rest of the South was in trouble, the tariff was less to blame than three other major forces: the postwar depression; the exhaustion of the soil in the old coastal states which had sharply reduced cotton and tobacco crops; and cotton competition from the Southern territories farther west.

Soon after peace in 1815, the cost of Southern land had in many areas soared to $100 an acre and the cost of slaves to $1,000. Then the price of cotton fell; the 173 million pounds shipped to England in 1825 was double the total shipped six years earlier—but it was worth $600,000 less. By the mid-1820s the bottom had dropped out, and $100-an-acre land could not be sold for $20. Meanwhile, Southerners were further depleting their land by planting more and more cotton, because more money had to be found.

The tariff question was nothing new. There had been, in fact, a series of avowedly protective tariffs before 1828. One had been passed in 1816 and another in 1824. Now America's infant industries, almost all of them in the North, demanded even further tariff aid against overseas competition. But for much of the South the tariffs were disastrous. Cotton was sold on the open market, and Southerners for years had bought their manufactured goods inexpensively from England and Europe; the tariff forced them to buy high and to sell low. South Carolina was hit especially hard; a congressman from that

Entitled "The March of Death," this cautionary print of a skeleton draped with distilling apparatus was dedicated to U.S. temperance societies, which increased along with 19th Century consumption of alcohol. The societies at first tolerated fermented beers and wines, but soon began demanding total abstinence. Their first big victory came in 1846: Maine went dry.

Eli Whitney, fresh out of Yale, was a guest on the plantation of General Nathanael Greene's widow when he invented the cotton gin in 1793. The simple device (below), whose toothed cylinders separated seeds from cotton, did the work of 50 slaves. It was widely pirated, and in many long legal battles Whitney was awarded only a small fraction of the invention's worth.

state, George McDuffie, asserted in 1830 that 40 out of every 100 bales of cotton were being figuratively plundered by Northern manufacturing interests. There was a very strong feeling in the region that something had to be done, and revolutionary resistance was being talked about. This was the situation that confronted Calhoun.

Whatever his understanding of economics, the political implications were perfectly clear. Calhoun himself had supported that first tariff of 1816. Eager to advance the general welfare of the nation, and convinced that his state would someday develop manufactures, he had promoted the special interests of new industries. "Neither agriculture, manufactures, nor commerce, taken separately, is the cause of wealth," he had said then. "It flows from the three combined." Now, it turned out, the tariff was not merely helping a special group, but was injurious to others, and thus to the general welfare. Calhoun understood the troubles of the Southern farmers and planters at firsthand, for he was a working farmer himself.

Something was tragically wrong with America, he believed, when a combined geographical interest could disregard the general welfare and turn an important local interest to its own profit. Examining the dilemma in 1828, Calhoun first asked himself whether there was any way out in the Constitution—a veto power, perhaps, that would enable his oppressed state to free itself from the tariff entirely? Power, he knew, could be opposed only by power. Night after night he struggled with the problem as, from across the state and beyond it, men besieged him with pleas to find a way out. He had little rest that summer, even after the visitors had picked their way across the shaded gallery of his home, through the litter of children's toys and hound dogs, and the carriage wheels had rolled away into the night.

For Calhoun knew (and was haunted by the knowledge) that South Carolina was splitting into two armed camps. Die-hard Unionists were massed on the one hand, fire-eating states'-righters on the other. When they clashed, the impact would extend far beyond South Carolina. It might even mean civil war. As the foremost man in the state, his was the task of reconciling the dissidents, of finding a practical substitute for the submission of the Unionists and the defiance of the Secessionists, of finding a peaceful way out. And the answer that came to him, as he paced his porch in South Carolina and pondered in his nearby office, was nullification, a doctrine the nation would come to know well in the two decades to come.

NULLIFICATION did not originate with Calhoun, although he carried it further than anyone else ever had. Actually the doctrine was evolved by Thomas Jefferson and James Madison in the Kentucky and Virginia Resolutions of 1798 and 1799. If Congress passed laws which the states considered unconstitutional, Jefferson said, the states had the power to decide if the measures were "unauthoritative, void, and of no force," and to determine what to do. "Nullification," he said, "is the rightful remedy." Madison said that the states together could "interpose" themselves between their citizens and unauthorized federal power, but Jefferson went further. The right of nullification, he said, was held by the legislature of each single state.

So, too, thought Calhoun. Under nullification as he viewed it, a single state should be able to veto, within its own borders, a federal law that it deemed unconstitutional—subject to the later approval of at least one fourth of the states. If such approval was not forthcoming, the state should, if it wished, be allowed to secede from the Union.

For the South, the implications of this principle were obvious. Nowhere in the Constitution was Congress given the express right to impose a tariff whose purpose was simply to protect industry. Under nullification, therefore, the South could ignore the tariff as if it did not exist. This was "states' rights" carried to the ultimate degree—and it promised a Southern solution not only to the region's economic dilemma but to the antislavery threat as well.

Having found his answer in nullification, Calhoun moved carefully. The issue was sure to arouse controversy, and Calhoun could not now afford controversy. Calhoun was a Vice President who hoped for election to the presidency—like Jefferson 30 years earlier—and he needed support from all over the country. Jefferson's authorship of the Kentucky documents had been kept secret for years. And the "Exposition and Protest," which Calhoun secretly wrote during that hot summer of 1828, was not credited to him when the South Carolina legislature issued it later in the year. Nevertheless, it was his. In it, he flatly declared that with certain qualifications any state could nullify any federal law it regarded as unconstitutional. This was the first step in his drive to rally his entire section of the country—now indirectly, later directly and eloquently—to make a last stand for its agricultural civilization and against high protective tariffs and industrial democracy.

Fort Hill, John C. Calhoun's home in South Carolina, served as a rendezvous for nullification leaders in 1832. The mansion, now a part of the Clemson College campus, overlooked a plantation of 550 acres worked by 80 or 90 slaves. The land was so rich it almost returned a profit despite depressed farm prices and Calhoun's innumerable long absences at the political wars.

MORE than at any time since his young manhood, Calhoun was at this period one with his own people. In 1825 he had "come home" after his long years in Washington, and had struck his roots deep into the red earth from which he had sprung. High in the up-country—with its old fieldstone churches and long corncribs and barns, with the dusty blue hills shouldering against the sky—he had purchased a farm. He loved it all: the winds from the mountains whipping through the cedar trees that bordered his drive, the heady scent of the box hedges and the spiciness of his favorite mimosa, the pears ripening in the sun and the cornbread soaking in sorghum, the creaking of the crickets on a summer's night and the singing of the peepers in the spring, the white stars of the dogwood, the swaying rhythm of a wheat field and the bloom of the cotton flowers, and the rivers, slow and pink in the summer and a silvery rush in the spring.

There can be no understanding of Calhoun without understanding his love of the land. Out of this had sprung his love of country and his dream of America as the perfect state. Daniel Webster had some of the same feeling, with his cattle and horses at his own beloved Marshfield in Massachusetts. But Calhoun farmed for a living, as well as for pleasure. His family was large. He had worked with his hands as a boy and now, in the Jeffersonian tradition, was happily inventing a subsoil plow and experimenting with plaster of Paris as a fertilizer. He worked from dawn to dark in his fields, returning to his house hot, tired, dirty and happy. He wanted to keep this life inviolate, and it was being threatened.

Calhoun at 46 was very different from what he had been during his years as congressman and Secretary of War. He was now possessed by a kind of apostolic zeal. Young men found him fascinating as he voiced his ideas in abrupt, emphatic phrases, yet there was a gentleness in him that was especially winning to women and children. He was more striking looking than ever, leaner,

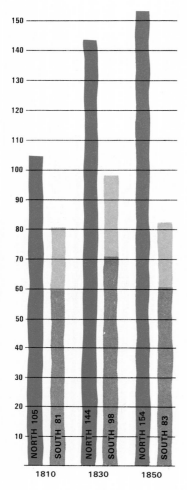

VOTES IN CONGRESS,
NORTH VERSUS SOUTH

This graph compares the North's congressional representation (blue bars) with that of the 14 Southern and border states (brown) over a 40-year span. Since the Constitution based apportionment on "the whole Number of free Persons," plus "three-fifths of all other Persons," nonvoting Negro slaves increased the South's representation by about a third (shown in tan). Nevertheless the South lost ground in the House. Its strength there approached the North's in 1810. But by 1850, representatives of the fast-growing North outnumbered the South's almost two to one.

his dark eyes shining more brilliantly beneath the bushy brows. But a foreign visitor thought him like a highly wrought piece of machinery set going by a weight, and to some he was coming to seem more of "a mental and moral abstraction" than a man. By 1840 a friend would find him so overstimulating that he could stand him only as "an occasional companion [for] when I seek relaxation with him, he screws me only the higher in some sort of excitement." One visitor, who spent some three hours trying to follow Calhoun's close reasoning through "heaven and earth," suddenly burst out: "I hate a man who makes me think so much."

Now Calhoun had brought his power and intellect to bear upon a single question. Years before he had told Charles Stewart, a naval hero of the War of 1812, that when the South ceased to control the government it would "resort to the dissolution of the union." The prospect dismayed him, for he loved his country. In 1821 John Quincy Adams had written in his diary: "Calhoun is a man . . . of ardent patriotism. He is above all sectional and factious prejudices, more than any other statesman of this Union with whom I have ever acted." Now, goaded and driven, he began his hopeless quest to reconcile irreconcilables, to hold together the past and the future.

THE issue came to a head dramatically, unexpectedly, in a Senate debate in which Vice President Calhoun, as presiding officer, could not even take part. The principal adversaries, in that early winter of 1830, were Daniel Webster of Massachusetts and South Carolina's Robert Young Hayne, and their contest was to go down as one of the great debates of United States history. Ostensibly, the subject under discussion was the disposal of the public lands, that simmering question which had boiled up during John Quincy Adams' presidency and had sputtered on ever since. At the beginning, Webster and Hayne seemed to be on the same side; that is, both favored the public lands bill. The only question seemed to be, in whose interests were the public lands to be plundered? New England millowners feared they would have to raise their pay scales if too much free public land was opened up, because their workers could then go west. The South feared the admission of more states which might become free and vote against Southern interests.

No such fears troubled the chief advocate of the public lands. This was Thomas Hart Benton of Missouri, a huge hulk of a man with sloping shoulders, a Roman nose and a winning smile. In 1813 Benton had fought a tavern brawl with the young Andrew Jackson in defense of his brother and lived to tell about it; he later became Old Hickory's foremost supporter in the Senate. Vanity was Benton's hallmark, but it was at once so colossal and so childlike that it somehow failed to offend. "Baneton," as he pronounced it, was convinced that he *was* the people ("Benton and the people, Benton and Democracy are one and the same, sir, synonymous terms, sir"). Now he thrust out his chin and rolled his periods grandiloquently. It was "an injury to the whole human race," he declared, "to undertake to preserve the vast and magnificent valley of the Mississippi for the haunts of beasts and savages instead of making it the abode of liberty and civilization." What of the poor in the cities, who were forced to labor at low wages in the East, when they might be enjoying a healthful agricultural life in the unsettled lands of the West? Slowly, as the debate of the legislators ground on, the issue shifted from public lands to tariffs, and a new tension hung in the air.

There was something majestic about the Senate in those days. As Sam Houston observed of the body in 1837, there was "no hum, no noise, no whispering." Men listened. While the 1830 debate proceeded, two men listened with special interest. One was the Vice President, deeply concerned about the tariff question. The other was Webster, the legendary "Black Dan," with his splendid domed forehead, his lustrous eyes and solid, stately form.

No one, it was said, could be quite so great as Daniel Webster looked. His costume resembled that of a Revolutionary soldier—the buff-colored vest and the dark blue coat with the brass buttons. He had a somber magnificence and, when he spoke, a quietly intense quality of drama.

He had come a long way from his beginnings in the lonely farm country near the headwaters of the Merrimack, and from his teen-age school days when at the weekly session devoted to public speaking he "could never command sufficient resolution" to rise and declaim. Later, at Dartmouth, he had developed skill in debate. Now he was one of the greatest orators in the land. Whereas Calhoun could excite the minds, and Clay could touch the hearts, of their listeners, Webster could stir men with an inspiration that was equaled by no other speaker of his time.

In his early congressional days, Webster had criticized the War of 1812, suggesting that individual states could nullify a federal law by "the solemn duty of the State Governments . . . to interpose between their citizens and arbitrary power." Now this son of New Hampshire, who was a senator from Massachusetts but symbolized all New England, stood forward as spokesman for an entire and undivided Union.

It was Benton who had shifted the subject of the debate on public lands to the sectional issues that were disturbing the nation. The attempt to limit Western settlement, said Benton, was "a most complex scheme of injustice, which taxes the South to injure the West, to pauperize the poor of the North." Hayne took up the refrain. Handsome, blond and youthful, Hayne was a practiced speaker—one of the very few at the time equipped to meet Webster on anything approaching equal terms. He touched on regional issues only briefly. Then the dimensions of his argument suddenly widened, and he launched into a stinging attack upon the dangers of "consolidation"—i.e., strengthening—of the Federal Union. Sale of the public lands, he cried, would give further power to the national government, which was already far too strong.

Brilliant Representative George McDuffie, one of South Carolina's most radical nullifiers, suffered from dyspepsia and a dueling bullet lodged against his spine. As if to relieve the pain, he made sensational speeches full of rancor and abuse. His "gloomy churlishness" increased until he finally went mad.

WEBSTER sensed danger. When debate resumed the next day he took the floor. "Consolidation," he declared contemptuously, "that perpetual cry, both of terror and delusion. . . . The union of the States will be strengthened by whatever furnishes inducements to the people . . . to hold together." Certainly this was no time "to calculate the value of the Union."

Hayne responded. Webster's words had rankled, he said, and he wanted to return the shot. Webster rose and folded his arms over his broad chest. "I am ready to receive it," he said.

Eloquently, Hayne insisted that he was defending both South Carolina and the Union. By suggesting a constitutional method of protest—that is, nullification—the legislature of South Carolina was *safeguarding* the Union. To permit the federal government to judge its own powers, the senator argued, would reduce the states to impotence. In that case a simple numerical majority, half a continent away, could impose its will on the South and reduce it to ruin.

Ironically Robert Young Hayne, a famous orator in his time, is chiefly remembered as the man who provoked Daniel Webster's greatest speech (opposite). Hayne resigned from the Senate in 1832; fellow South Carolinian Calhoun, who as Vice President was barred from debate, took Hayne's place.

How could any such government call itself free? "Who, then," Hayne asked, "are the friends of the Union?" And he supplied his own answer: "Those who would confine the Federal Government strictly within the limits prescribed by the constitution. . . . And who are its enemies? Those who are in favor of consolidation; who are constantly stealing power from the States, and adding strength to the Federal Government."

The day Webster rose for his second speech, the Senate Chamber bloomed like a flower garden even though it was the coldest day of the winter. A great ₊rowd had come to hear him, and colorfully dressed ladies filled the galleries and even occupied some senators' chairs.

His organlike voice filling the room, Webster outlined his vision of the Union, his left hand behind him, his right moving up and down. It was his most splendid hour, and no one who heard or saw him on that day would ever forget it. This address alone, printed and scattered across the country, made him unquestionably the first man in Congress.

He reduced the question to basic constitutional terms. Was the national government the creation of the states, or was it the agent of the people? It was his belief that the primary aim of the Constitutional Convention had been to set up a government not subject to the whims of the original 13 states. "It is, sir," he addressed Calhoun, the presiding officer, "the people's Constitution, the people's government, made for the people, made by the people, and answerable to the people." It was absurd, Webster said, to suggest "Liberty first and Union afterwards" as a motto for America. And then he cried out, in words the nation has never forgotten: "Liberty *and* Union, now and forever, one and inseparable!"

When it was all over, the Webster-Hayne debate had settled nothing, but it had brought into the open the issue that men would be debating for the next 30 years. Webster's silent antagonist in the Vice President's chair well knew that this occasion was simply the start of a tremendous struggle. The South Carolina doctrine would not be downed that easily.

JACKSON had not yet been heard from. Southerners saw a possibility in that spring of 1830 that he might denounce the tariff, or even endorse nullification. They decided to smoke the President out. The occasion was the first Jefferson Birthday dinner, held on April 13, 1830, in Washington. The toasts, most of them nullificationist, were printed up in advance. The Marine Band played. Jackson and Calhoun attended—both, with their long angular heads and bushy hair, looming over the other diners. Finally, Jackson was called upon for an extemporaneous toast. He stood, drew his tall form erect, looked directly at Calhoun and said: "Our Union. It must be preserved."

With the issue so bluntly stated, Calhoun rose to the challenge. But his eyes had gone black and his hand trembled. Slowly, he replied: "The Union—next to our liberty, the most dear. May we always remember that it can only be preserved by distributing equally the benefits and burdens of the Union."

That same spring, relations between the President and Vice President suffered another disastrous blow from which they never recovered. In a letter he received from former Secretary of the Treasury William H. Crawford, Jackson learned to his surprise that 12 years before, when Monroe's Cabinet had discussed the general's highhanded forays in Florida, Secretary of War Calhoun, far from defending Jackson, had favored punishing him. Calhoun had never admitted this to Jackson. Jackson now sent him Crawford's letter with a note asking if it was true. Calhoun avoided a direct reply, and Jackson exploded. He shot back a last note to Calhoun. "Understanding you now," he said bitterly, "no further communication with you on this subject is necessary." The break between the two was final by 1831.

Without Jackson's support, Calhoun's chances for the presidency were dead, and he knew it. Thus far he had not openly advocated the doctrine of nullification. But on July 26, 1831, from his home in South Carolina, Calhoun issued a statement—later known as the Fort Hill Address—openly advocating the controversial principle for the first time. In a widely publicized letter to the South Carolina governor he amplified his views. Nullification was both a peaceable and constitutional avenue of dissent, he said; the Constitution was merely an agreement reached among the separate states, and each of them was free to interpret the compact in its own way. He had leveled a challenge which the nation could not ignore.

EVENTS were now moving toward a climax. In December 1831, Jackson made the conciliatory recommendation that tariffs be reduced, and Congress followed his suggestion in July 1832. But Southerners were not appeased; they felt the new rates were still too high.

That autumn South Carolina dramatically moved to put Calhoun's philosophy into effect. A special convention meeting in Columbia passed an ordinance nullifying the United States tariff acts of 1828 and 1832, and prohibiting the collection of duties within the state. The legislature in turn voted to raise an army. Unionists and nullifiers alike marched with banners and flags, and Charleston rang with the toast, "Nullification—the only rightful remedy of an injured state." Expressing the growing bitterness of his area, Congressman George McDuffie went further; he called the Union a "foul monster."

Jackson was furious. Even his friends were shocked as he threatened to "hang every leader . . . of that infatuated people, sir, by martial law, irrespective of his name, or political or social position." There was no mistaking that he meant the Vice President. Jackson ran for re-election in that autumn of 1832—but without Calhoun, who was planning a return to the Senate. The President won overwhelmingly, but nullification was never very far from his thoughts. After the election he told some visitors: "The best thing about this, gentlemen, is that it strengthens my hands in this trouble." Still, he said nothing in public. At last, on December 10, came the most significant of all his state papers, his "Proclamation to the People of South Carolina." The words roused the country.

"The Constitution . . . forms a *government*, not a league," Jackson declared. To annul a law was "incompatible with the existence of the Union," and "to say that any State may at pleasure secede . . . is to say that the United States is not a nation." He made it perfectly clear that to him nullification and secession meant the same thing and both meant war.

In South Carolina his appeal fell on deaf ears. By the end of December, Hayne had resigned from the Senate and was now governor. Calhoun was now senator. South Carolina stood ready to repel force by force.

Jackson, too, was ready. He instructed the Secretary of War to report how many arms were ready for the field; he had already ordered 5,000 muskets to Castle Pinckney in Charleston Harbor, along with a sloop of war and seven

EXCERPTS FROM WEBSTER'S
FAMOUS REPLY TO HAYNE

I profess, Sir, in my career hitherto, to have kept steadily in view the preservation of our Federal Union. It is to that Union we owe our safety at home, and our dignity abroad. It has been to us all a copious fountain of national, social, and personal happiness. I have not allowed myself, Sir, to look beyond the Union, to see what might lie hidden in the dark recess behind. While the Union lasts we have high, exciting, gratifying prospects spread out before us, for us and our children. Beyond that I seek not to penetrate the veil.

When my eyes shall be turned to behold for the last time the sun in heaven, may I not see him shining on the broken and dishonored fragments of a once glorious Union. Let their last feeble glance rather behold the gorgeous ensign of the republic, now known and honored throughout the earth, still full high advanced, not a stripe erased or polluted, nor a single star obscured, bearing for its motto, no such miserable interrogatory as "What is all this worth?" nor those other words of delusion and folly, "Liberty first and Union afterwards," but everywhere, spread all over in characters of living light, blazing on all its ample folds, as they float over the sea and over the land, and in every wind under the whole heavens, that other sentiment, dear to every true American heart—Liberty and Union, now and forever, one and inseparable!

revenue cutters. He dispatched a special secret agent to Charleston to find out just how far the rebellious state might go.

What is most remarkable is the caution with which the supposedly inflammatory general moved during these tense weeks. He knew that the country was not completely behind him. Many loyal Americans still believed in the abstract right of secession. The Hartford Convention, in which certain New England delegates had espoused doctrines very much like nullification, had taken place only 17 years before. Even Daniel Webster had once wondered openly if the President had a right to blockade Charleston or to call out troops for the purpose of putting down nullification before any overt act of hostility occurred in the state.

But Jackson continued to move with admirable restraint. Although in private he talked angrily of hanging Calhoun, he made it clear publicly that only if South Carolina tried to force the issue would he act. "In 40 days," he had announced, "I can have within the limits of South Carolina 50,000 men." If it was known that he could and would do so, it would not need to be done.

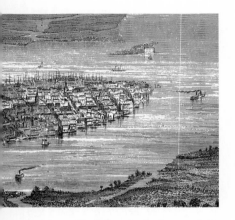

Charleston, the focal point of the nullification struggle, fills a peninsula where, according to an old local witticism, "The Ashley (bottom) and Cooper (top) Rivers come together to form the Atlantic Ocean." Beyond, on the island marked "4," stands Castle Pinckney (far right, below). To this fort President Jackson sent his 1832 warning to rebels—a large shipment of arms.

ON January 4, 1833, Calhoun entered the Senate Chamber to take the oath. It was for Calhoun the supreme ordeal of his life. His trip up from South Carolina was something like a journey to his own execution. It was widely believed Jackson would seize him on his arrival. He was stared at and shunned; old acquaintances refused to take his hand. Not since Aaron Burr had there been such intensity of feeling about a public figure. But as he calmly took his oath to protect and defend the Constitution of the United States, the tension relaxed a little and several who had hung back came up to greet him.

On January 16, Jackson's so-called Force Bill, calling for arms to put down resistance in South Carolina, was sent to Congress. The instant it was read, Calhoun was on his feet, impassioned and defiant. Indignantly, he spurned the charge that either he or his state favored disunion; Southerners applauded; his words, said a future President, John Tyler of Virginia, were "warm—impassioned, burning." Tyler exulted: "Rely upon it, he is more than a match for all opponents."

On January 22, Calhoun introduced some resolutions contending that the federal system joined "free and independent States in a bond of union for mutual advantages," and that it could be preserved in either of two ways—by the consent of its members or by "a government of the sword." He followed up with a major address on February 15. Once again—in short, sparse sentences —he defended South Carolina and its doctrine and denounced the Force Bill as a measure of war.

For two days Calhoun held the floor. When he had finished, Webster rose. The Constitution, he said, was not a compact between sovereign states who might secede from it, but "an executed contract" among a people to set up a permanent government. "The people of the United States are one people," Webster declared. "They are one in making war, and one in making peace; they are one in regulating commerce, and one in laying duties." He, at least, was tired of denunciations of majority rule. "What, then, do gentlemen wish? Do they wish to establish a *minority* government?" For four hours the Massachusetts senator spoke with all his old power, and his words echoed across the land.

Calhoun was not yet beaten. On February 26, he once again presented a closely reasoned exposition of his view that the Constitution was indeed a compact. He spoke for two hours, rallying the old arguments but with new fervor. The Senate listened in fascination, and it was widely agreed that he had bested Webster. Calhoun himself thought so. When somebody briefly obscured John Randolph's view of the events, he said: "Take away that hat. I want to see Webster die, muscle by muscle."

Yet in the end, there could be only one victor. Calhoun spoke for the past, for an era when the desires of individual states could be paramount. But Webster spoke for the future and the kind of union in which a great nationalistic democracy could thrive. Inevitably his ideas, not Calhoun's, would prevail.

Debate could settle the nullification issue, but it could not settle rebellion. In Charleston the militia was parading in review. Jackson's finger lay lightly on a hair trigger. Men could march and sing to their hearts' content, but the minute South Carolina acted he would move.

"These South Carolinians are good fellows, and it would be a pity to let Jackson hang them," a senator remarked to Henry Clay. The Kentuckian agreed. Clay had saved the Union once before, and he was contemplating moving into action now. For weeks he had had the draft of a compromise tariff in his desk, but he had hesitated to submit it, uncertain of its reception.

But evidence was mounting that a compromise would be welcomed. On February 12 Clay brought his bill forward. Calhoun immediately gave it his backing. "He who loves the Union must desire to see this agitating question brought to a termination," he told the Senate. The galleries rocked with applause. The compromise tariff slipped through in less than a month, but Jackson still had the last word. His Force Bill to compel the submission of South Carolina was rammed through the Senate on February 20. Every Southern senator but one stalked out in protest behind the defiant Calhoun.

Calhoun still had his biggest battle before him. He had to ride to South Carolina, night and day in stages and open mail coaches, to convince the rebellious state that nullification meant civil war. He arrived in time to persuade the state's leaders. South Carolina turned from open outcries for secession to the empty gesture of nullifying the Force Bill. Calhoun, drained physically and emotionally, retreated to Fort Hill. "The struggle, so far from being over," he wrote, "is not more than fairly commenced."

Safely ensconced on her vine-clad piazza, a plantation belle expresses opposition to the federal tariff by sewing onto a gentleman's hat a blue cockade with a palmetto button. But Southerners were far from unanimous for nullification. While belligerent menfolk fought partisan brawls and duels, some women were displaying American eagles as a symbol of unionist sympathy.

THREE men had saved the Union in this first major challenge to its authority: Henry Clay, who offered and pushed through the compromise settlement; Calhoun, who dealt with the South Carolina extremists—and Jackson. Jackson's show of force and scorn of appeasement were object lessons to the entire South. "I met nullification at its threshold," he wrote James Buchanan, who unfortunately forgot this in his own hour of reckoning as President in 1860-1861. And in another letter Jackson answered in one sentence the question that was one day to torment Lincoln: "If the governor of Virginia should have the folly to prevent the militia from marching through his State . . . I would arrest him at the head of his troops."

And Calhoun—had it not been for nullification, the "rightful remedy" that he advocated, South Carolina might well have resorted to secession and civil war. Calhoun was convinced—if Jackson was not—that nullification was the palliative, not the cause of the excitement. And if South Carolina seceded, other Southern states might well have followed her down a darkening path.

A diligent search for the good life

INSPIRED by the certainty that theirs was a nation going places, Americans in the first half of the 19th Century labored eagerly to improve their lot. Optimism was the spirit of the day. It sometimes seemed that any man who failed at farming promptly turned to banking; if he failed again, he turned to the law, knowing that he had not yet tried mining. If he could not find success in one town, he tried elsewhere; visitors to America remarked on the people's readiness to cast off community ties in search of a better tomorrow. "Men change their houses, their climate, their trade, their condition, their party, their sect," exclaimed a Frenchman. In their search for the good life, farmers, businessmen and consumers bought heavily on credit. They ran up staggering bills *(opposite)*, but they forged ahead even when the credit pyramid collapsed in the crashes of 1837 and 1839. For Americans were sure that they lived in the best of all possible worlds and that, despite momentary setbacks, the United States was on the road to the greatest prosperity the world had ever known.

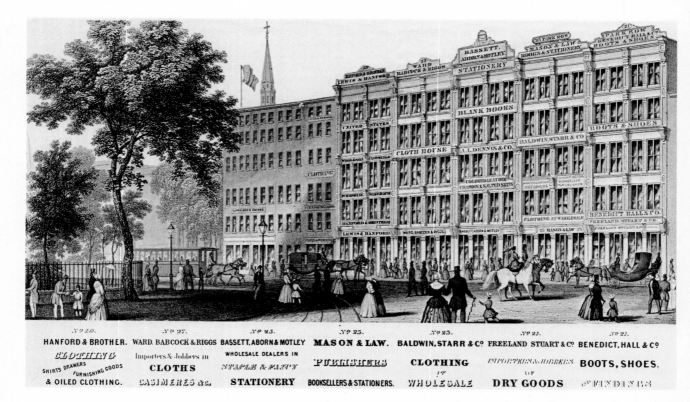

NEW SHOPS advertising ready-made products are shown in a lithograph of New York's Park Row in the 1850s. They were built by John Jacob Astor, reputedly the nation's richest man.

"THE LONG BILL" by James H. Beard illustrates the plight of a general store customer of the 1830s, trapped between the lure of abundant goods and the hard reality of rising prices.

Days on the farm: hard work and a happy buzz of "bees"

THE occupation that engaged the majority of Americans for most of the 19th Century was agriculture, although a national decline in the percentage of farmers had been under way for some time. In 1820 some 72 per cent of the American workers, both slave and free, were on farms; by 1850 the ratio had dropped to 64 per cent. The number of farm workers in the North and West was roughly equal to the total in the South, but working conditions were far different: even the most prosperous of Northern farmers customarily labored in their own fields. The hard work—along with the low income—was certainly one reason why an increasing number of young Northerners drifted away from the rural areas to the cities to seek jobs.

Yet none could say that life on the farm was all rigor. When major tasks had to be undertaken, neighbors came from miles around to help. The result was the "bee," a community effort whose name seems to have originated in America. There were husking bees, apple bees, quilting bees, cellar-digging bees, even kissing bees. For obvious reasons, bees also were known as "frolics." The editor of a farmers' almanac warned in 1816: "Husking is now a business for us all. If you make what some call a *Bee*, it will be necessary to keep an eye on the boys, or you may have to husk over again the whole heap."

A QUILTING BEE, devoted as much to gossip as to work, is held in the warmth of an iron stove, a luxury that began to supplant the fireplace in the 1830s. Such bees often went on for days.

A HAYING BEE in Massachusetts awaits refreshment as a top-hatted farmer makes his way across the field *(right)* with jug and hamper for his co-workers. Part of the main house, 60 years old when this picture was painted in 1825, still stands in Southbridge.

A SCUTCHING BEE brigade in Pennsylvania gets some flax ready to be woven into linen. Scutching was a beating process which separated the flax from the woody fiber. The worker at the left is crushing the stalks in a "flax brake" to prepare them for scutching.

A fine display of farm riches

A Pennsylvania fair in the year 1824 affords farmers an opportunity to study methods for improving their crops and livestock. Small landholders often resisted such advances as crop rotation and new machinery, notwithstanding the availability of helpful farm journals, but gentlemen farmers proved more

willing to experiment. Henry Clay, for example, imported the first Hereford cattle to the United States in 1817. The county fair, an important stimulus to good farming, had its beginnings in Massachusetts, where in 1810 a wealthy Pittsfield man named Elkanah Watson organized a fair so local farmers could display their livestock. By 1850 farm fairs had become regular events in New York, Pennsylvania and Ohio. The above scene, done in primitive style by a local sign painter, shows implements *(fore-ground)* for plowing, hoeing and raking. Farmers inspect live-stock while colleagues compete in a plowing contest *(rear, left)*.

Fads and fancies in the city

As the cities grew they graphically reflected the temperaments of their residents. Philadelphia was quiet, New York commercial, Boston culture-minded—and all were self-satisfied. British writer Frederick Marryat noted in 1839 that "Boston turns up her erudite nose at New York; Philadelphia, in her pride, looks down upon both New York and Boston; while New York, chinking her dollars, swears the Bostonians are a parcel of pu-

The very latest styles from Paris are displayed in a fashion plate.

In a prosperous Boston restaurant of 1840, businessmen enjoy the popular new "quick lunch."

New Yorkers trim excess at Dr. Rich's Institute. Gymnasiums prospered in the 1800s.

A boy peddles a New York daily. Price: one penny.

Patrons relax in an ice cream parlor, which sold ice cream, ice water—and ice.

Cashing in on the current lecture fad, meteorologist

ritanical prigs, and the Philadelphians a would-be aristocracy."

In a fast-changing environment Americans were still groping for a distinctive culture. The embodiment of this process was New York, which by 1810 had become the nation's largest city —and also the rowdiest, most fashion conscious and (some visitors thought) the most vulgar. Entertainment—concerts, the theater, horse racing, lecture-going—was already big business in this bustling metropolis. People had money to spend and they often spent it ostentatiously. The fashionable women of the East "show half their revenue in silks and satins," sniffed the English traveler Mrs. Frances Trollope. The spectacle that so fascinated and appalled visitors from abroad had a fairly simple explanation. New York, like the other cities of America, had merely entered the awkward age of adolescence.

Americans dance the polka, in sympathy with Europe's revolutions.

Racing for a $20,000 purse, horses near the finish at a course on Long Island.

A farce plays to a full house in New York in 1822.

A New York neighborhood milkman of the '40s makes deliveries.

James Pollard Espy addresses a New York group in 1841.

Julia Gardiner, future wife of President Tyler, endorses a shop in an ad.

An 1844 advertisement features indoor plumbing, for the rich only.

The bustling confusion of a nation on the move

THE unsettled nature of life in mid-century America was nowhere better illustrated than in the nation's housing habits. Newfangled gadgets were coming along so fast, and the standard of living rising so swiftly, that almost everybody aspired to live in a newer, fancier, more expensive place than the one he was occupying. Indoor plumbing, stoves, ready-made furniture, even ready-made houses appeared on the scene. Philadelphia boasted 2,000 indoor baths. Concrete ("unaffected by the action of the weather") was introduced as a building material. Prefabricated dwellings were shipped from the East Coast to Texas. On moving day whole cities seemed to shift on their foundations. People who liked their houses but not their locations had no hesitation about moving the houses. Charles Dickens wrote in astonishment that he once met a house "coming downhill at a good round trot, drawn by some twenty oxen!"

FURNITURE BUYERS inspect factory-made pieces, alert to changing fashions. The elegant sneered at colonial furniture as a sign of poverty and shunted Windsor chairs to the kitchen.

FURNITURE MOVERS create bedlam in New York on moving day. On May 1, the traditional upheaval date, advancing rents and advancing tastes whipped the populace into a frenzy—"as if alarmed by some extensive conflagration," wrote an Englishman. The artist who painted this picture remained sufficiently poised, however, to insert himself with palette *(lower left)*.

The tardy campaign against fire, filth and crime

AMERICAN cities mushroomed so quickly in the early 19th Century that public services were, for all practical purposes, left to the gods to provide. Philadelphia, an exception, installed an adequate water system as early as 1801 but New York did not follow suit until 1842. Even those water services that replaced the corner pump did not eliminate visible impurities; a visitor to Chicago complained of "chowder" in his bathtub.

No uniformed police existed until the 1850s, when New York—and later Philadelphia and Boston—decided that a badge was not sufficient identification. Americans complained that a policeman would not arrest a thief unless he was bribed to do so. Fires, the worst scourge of the cities, were fought by enthusiastic volunteers who, racing through the night with their clothes tucked under their arms, vied to reach the scene first. Upon arriving, they dressed, then often fought pitched battles for first place while the fire raged unchecked. Except in Philadelphia and a few smaller towns, garbage collection remained the province of hordes of pigs and packs of dogs that roamed the streets. No mass transit existed till New York ran a coach up Broadway in 1830.

WELCOMING WATER, crowds gather as Boston inaugurates its water system in 1848. A fountain spouted, the militia marched and children sang James Russell Lowell's ode starting "My name is Water."

FIGHTING A FIRE, Brooklyn marines and firemen from New Haven and Philadelphia join New York volunteers in battling to subdue the blaze that swept through lower Manhattan in December of 1835.

The warmth of family life

Gracious living is epitomized by a charming family scene painted in Hartford in 1836. Although the family's members are now anonymous, their portrait (which the artist humorously painted over and over again above the mantel) discloses much about them. That they were well-to-do is evident from the fine wall-

paper and the wool carpet. The boy doing his homework was one of the relatively few young men fortunate enough to receive an education; as late as 1860 only one out of six white children in the North attended school. Despite the warmth of this scene, Europeans often described American families as "cold and formal." But one Polish visitor disagreed. American ways, said Count Adam de Gurowski, were "misunderstood or not thoroughly examined" by critical foreigners. The fact is, he wrote, "Americans stand out best in the simple domesticity of family life. . . . [Their] homes are warmed by parental love."

33

2. THE PRESIDENT EMBATTLED

ALTHOUGH the most remarkable thing about the Administration of Andrew Jackson was the political impact of the man himself, his term in office saw a strange series of running engagements in the social arena in which the doughty general was soundly defeated. These encounters, the only battles he ever lost, revolved around the figure of a woman.

Jackson's interest in Peggy O'Neale was chivalrous, not romantic. She was the wife of his Secretary of War, John Henry Eaton. He was a distinguished lawyer and author, a man of culture and charm, but as far as the ladies of official society were concerned his wife was something else again. Her sins were various. She was young; she was pretty; she was a tavern keeper's daughter. Furthermore, her first husband, it was rumored, had cut his throat while at sea, and she was commonly reputed to have been the mistress of Secretary Eaton before she became a Cabinet lady. These were put forward as reasons for excluding the white-skinned, dark-haired Irish beauty from official society.

Jackson was furious. What touched him on the raw was the bitter memory of his own wife Rachel, hounded to her death by gossips. Had Rachel lived to enter the White House, he knew she too would have been the target of social slander. Would Andrew Jackson suffer this to happen to another woman under his protection? Not while there was breath left in his body.

The President battled his Cabinet on Peggy's behalf until all attempts to hold meetings were abandoned. He wrote to his friends; he raged against his

THE AUSTERE NEW ENGLANDER John Quincy Adams stands before his desk and an imaginary garden in this scene, painted a year after he had left the White House.

enemies; he told his Cabinet that Mrs. Eaton was "chaste as a virgin." Nothing helped. At balls "cotillion after cotillion dissolved into its original elements" when the beautiful Mrs. Eaton was placed at its head. The wife of the minister from Holland walked out of an official party when she found Peggy seated next to her at dinner; enraged, Jackson swore he would demand the recall of her husband. According to legend, Jackson visited Mrs. Calhoun, wife of the Vice President, and ordered her to return Mrs. Eaton's call on the theory that the rest of Washington society would follow her lead. The imperious little lady from Charleston, the story goes, ordered the President out of the house.

In the end a more designing politician, Martin Van Buren, solved the presidential dilemma. Secretary of State Van Buren was a widower, and so was able to disregard the Cabinet wives and entertain Mrs. Eaton. The son of a New York tavern keeper, Van Buren had for years been a member of the "Albany Regency," the successors in power to Aaron Burr's Tammany Hall machine. "Little Van" charted an unpredictable political course based on what his friends called his principles and his foes called mere goals of expediency. By some he was considered urbane and cynical, by others earnest and tactful. He "rowed to his object with muffled oars," observed John Randolph. Wily or well-meaning, he was in fact a born manipulator, who had developed the spoils system to perfection in New York as an excellent way to build a party machine on both the state and local level.

Seemingly, he was the last person on earth for Jackson to admire. He had come to Washington apparently planning to manipulate the President, but the tables were suddenly turned. Jackson's sense of politics was as keen as his ignorance of them, and in Van Buren he promptly recognized a master teacher. The two men meshed well, and Van Buren's careful kindness to Mrs. Eaton solidified his position with the President.

Van Buren's way out, face-saving for both Jackson and his antagonists, was to resign from the Cabinet in the certainty that his fellow members would follow suit. They did—and the President was able to start over again. Peggy Eaton's social aspirations were gratified when her husband was appointed ambassador to Spain. Van Buren's reward was the Court of St. James's in London. But on the Van Buren nomination there was a tie vote in the Senate—and Vice President Calhoun decided to ruin Van Buren politically by casting his own vote against the appointment. Gleefully the Vice President succumbed to the vernacular. "It will kill him, sir, kill him dead. . . ." Retorted Thomas Hart Benton: "You have broken a minister, and elected a Vice-President." And he was right.

The battle of Cabinet wives over Peggy Eaton (right), the tavern-owner's daughter whose husband was Secretary of War, grew until John Eaton frightened a fellow statesman out of town with guns. John Quincy Adams observed wryly that as betwixt conflicts he would "confine myself to the Russian and Turkish war." Mrs. John C. Calhoun (left) led the anti-Eatonites.

J ACKSON could now turn his attention to what would become the foremost issue of his entire Administration, the Bank of the United States. Even before his inauguration, Jackson had considered getting rid of the Bank. Basically, his grievance was what it had always been: that the Bank operated for the benefit of the rich few rather than for the many poor, and that it used public funds deposited with it to benefit special interest groups.

The Jacksonians—if not Jackson himself—had several other grievances, some avowedly political. The Bank had vast financial power; during the campaign of 1828, charges were made that several important branches had used their funds in an attempt to defeat Jackson. The Bank's president, Nicholas Biddle, who had personally voted for Jackson, denied the charges, and they were never proved. Yet Jackson men believed them, and they contributed greatly to the anti-Bank atmosphere within the Administration. Additional opposition from within the Administration came from men who were themselves connected with state banks and who saw in the Bank of the United States a powerful competitor.

Jackson's own suspicion of Eastern banking power was typical of the Western attitude of the time. Westerners strongly resented the East's financial monopoly, which denied them the cheap flow of paper money and easy credit that was so desirable in a farmer-debtor economy. Jackson himself, in a paper-money transaction with a Philadelphia merchant, had suffered a substantial loss that made him forever distrustful of Eastern financial interests. Furthermore he had often been forced to sell his own cotton, hogs and corn in New Orleans at sagging prices at the same time that he was buying merchandise in the East at high cost.

A well-known book of the time on paper money by William M. Gouge, an anti-Bank economist, depicts a classic cycle of boom and bust, in which the banks are cast as the villains: because they overissue their notes, prices rise; business overextends its credit, leading to overtrading; there is free spending, inflation and more notes are set afloat; and finally solid coin vanishes to pay debts abroad. Then comes a run on the banks, and panic, ending in nation-wide poverty and unemployment.

In this cartoon on the outcome of the Peggy Eaton dispute, all the Cabinet "rats" go scurrying off except Martin Van Buren, whose idea it was for them all to resign. He is being retained by the tail for greater things to come. This sketch prompted Van Buren's son John to joke that his father would return home from Washington "when the President takes his foot off!"

THOUGH the country was indeed vulnerable to this kind of collapse in the 1830s, and one eventually did occur, it was not solely the fault of the United States Bank, which on the whole had succeeded in doing what it set out to do. Its investments were prudent, its dividends high and it had given stability to the national economy. Ironically, the Bank was blamed most of all for doing what it was intended to do: tightening the credit and preventing an excess of paper money. It was blamed for things diametrically opposed to each other: in the East for issuing a limited amount of its own paper whose value fluctuated and thus kept prices paid by the workmen high; in the West for tight credit policies and high costs. It was blamed for inflation in the East and for deflation in the West, and for every conceivable banking evil in between.

Much of what it was blamed for was not really under its control. For one thing, the Bank was powerless to stop the Western banking practice of issuing huge amounts of inflationary paper money. Every so often, the Bank tried to control the situation by withholding credit from state banks and demanding payment in coin, thus reminding the "wildcat" banks that it had the power to put them out of business. This was good economics but poor politics, for it brought the accusation from Senator Benton that "all the flourishing cities of the West are mortgaged to this money power."

Like Jefferson, Jackson felt that widespread distribution of real property in dwellings and land safeguarded democracy, and that the Bank tended toward monopolistic control of American wealth by a single class. He also feared, erroneously, that foreigners owned enough American stock to control the country. Most important, he felt that the Bank was virtually in control of the nation. Although he planned to veto the bill renewing its charter, he was sure the Bank's power was so great that it would use government funds if need be to buy up the votes needed to override the veto. And it is true that the power of the Bank was actually so strong in Congress that the purchase of only a few additional votes would have been necessary to accomplish this end. In 1833 Biddle injudiciously boasted: "I can remove all the constitutional scruples in the District of Columbia." Jackson agreed. It was no secret that the Bank, and the business interests behind it, had found the value of making the right loans to the right congressmen at the right time. Daniel Webster was already financially influenced.

Jackson therefore declared that the Bank was unconstitutional, at odds with the general welfare, and had failed in its primary objective, to provide a sound currency. He dreamed of a kind of national bank of deposit, with wartime power to issue interest-bearing bills payable in peace. But he did not know how to create a money system that would not be prone to recurrent disaster. He may be forgiven this, for no one else has found such a system. In any event, Jackson believed to the end of his days that his war on the Bank was his crowning achievement as President. In taking it on, he fought far more than an institution. He also took on Senators Clay, Webster and Calhoun—and Nicholas Biddle.

A sleek and ingratiating charmer, scion of a distinguished Philadelphia family, Biddle was the outstanding financial autocrat of his day. He had been a child prodigy, a linguist, the author of a brilliant account of the Lewis and Clark expedition, and an able diplomat. Since 1823 he had been the highly competent head of the Bank and he may have fancied himself as another Hamilton. But he lacked the creative genius and political finesse of his great predecessor. It is true he was somewhat the victim of his tumultuous time. But although Biddle was not responsible for the rank electioneering of some branches of his Bank, he lacked the force to stop it.

Politically Nicholas Biddle was no match whatever for the old soldier in the White House. Biddle talked too much. He could and did say, "I have been for years in the daily exercise of more personal authority than any President habitually enjoys." He stupidly admitted that he could destroy state banks and create a depression: "Nothing but the evidence of suffering . . . will produce any effect in Congress." In short, he permitted himself to become intoxicated with his own power.

That was one mistake. His other was in heeding his friends Webster and Clay, who advised him to seek renewal of the Bank's charter four years before it was to expire in 1836. Should Jackson veto the measure, they contended,

Freed of the discipline of the Bank of the United States, local banks, business firms, even private persons issued uncontrolled quantities of penny-value paper money, such as the 50-cent note of a Baltimore savings fund at the right. People called them "shinplasters." Above, a figure from a mock shinplaster portrays President Jackson calling out for "more glory."

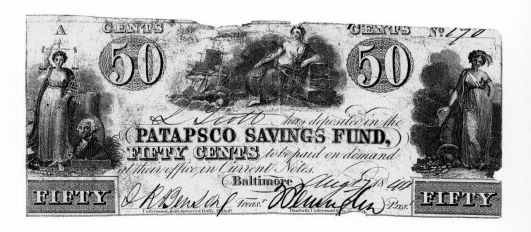

they would have a fighting issue for the 1832 presidential campaign. But they had roused a sleeping lion. Jackson's annual messages in 1830 and 1831 had scarcely mentioned the Bank. The recharter bill rallied him to battle. Van Buren, summoned to the White House after midnight, found the President in bed, wretchedly ill but with fire blazing in his eyes. The bill for recharter had been passed. Jackson slashed a veto across it and sent it back to Congress with a ringing message that aroused the fury of the Bank's supporters. Webster saw the veto message as seeking "to inflame the poor against the rich," and the Bank saw Webster in an even more favorable light than before, adding $10,000 to his outstanding loan of $22,000. Biddle commented: "This worthy President thinks that because he has scalped Indians . . . he is to have his way with the Bank." Biddle thought otherwise.

Although the Supreme Court had pronounced the Bank constitutional, Jackson disagreed. He was not disturbed in the slightest at finding himself at odds with the court. "Each officer who takes an oath to support the Constitution," he said blandly, "swears that he will support it as he understands it, and not as it is understood by others." To Biddle this was "a manifesto of anarchy."

The veto message was actually a resounding statement of Democratic policy—and a highly effective campaign document for 1832. Jackson denounced the Bank as a monopoly, "unauthorized by the Constitution, subversive of the rights of the States, and dangerous to the liberties of the people." He was aware that "equality of talents, of education, or of wealth" could not be produced by human institutions. But when "artificial distinctions" made the rich richer and the strong stronger, then the farmers, mechanics and laborers had a right to complain. Government must not let "the rich and powerful . . . [bend its acts] to their selfish purposes."

This was not nearly so revolutionary a pronouncement as its opponents tried to make it appear. As President, Jackson was not speaking for the West alone, or for any one grievance; he was not so much against bankers as against what he deemed a stifling monopoly. He knew that many, even in the East, felt concern over the powers and privileges of the Bank.

The President's veto was sustained, which sounded the opening gun for the 1832 presidential campaign. The National Republicans—soon to be called Whigs—had Henry Clay and a platform calling for internal improvements, declaring the Supreme Court to be the ultimate authority and asserting that

When Nicholas Biddle (below), the powerful head of the Bank of the United States, had his pocket picked in his own bank lobby, anti-Bank newspapers jeered that it was just a normal transaction at the Bank. Later, deprived of government deposits, his bank issued notes (left) based on cotton mortgages. When the price of cotton fell, Biddle almost went to jail.

Richard M. Johnson claimed he had killed Tecumseh in battle and campaigned for Vice President to the tune of "Rumpsey, Dumpsey, Colonel Johnson killed Tecumsey." Friends of Andrew Jackson, an authentic hero, said a lucky shot did not qualify a man for office. Jackson backed Johnson anyhow.

In a political satire based on a favorite nursery rhyme, the artist Edward Williams Clay pokes fun at the Jackson assault on the Bank. The cartoon contains many important figures, including Jackson's speechwriter Kendall and newspaper editor Blair. The "milkmaid" is believed to represent Peggy Eaton.

the removal of government servants who held opposing political views was an abuse of power. They also had the influential New York *Courier and Enquirer*, which abruptly deserted the Jackson-Van Buren ticket for Clay and the Bank. A subsequent congressional investigation revealed that money had played a large part in the paper's conversion.

The Democrats, formerly the Democratic Republicans, had Jackson and that was enough. All the old stories about him were revived, and there were cartoons depicting the President as a raving maniac or as a burglar trying to force the doors of the beautiful marble bank building. But the day of balloting came, and after it was over he had been re-elected overwhelmingly.

When Congress reconvened, Clay, who had thought a national bank unconstitutional back before the War of 1812 when he was against it, and had later discovered it was constitutional when he was for it, now declared: "I want to know where the Treasury of the United States is." For Jackson had decided to remove the government's deposits from the Bank and place them in state, or "pet," banks. This was unwise, especially as part of the arrangement involved turning the surplus federal funds over to the states. Some of the windfall wound up in the possession of the schools, but in Portsmouth, New Hampshire, it was given away to the voters, and in Guilford, New Hampshire, the selectmen simply helped themselves.

The uproar over the removal of the deposits was climaxed by the Senate's passage of Clay's resolution censuring the President. "Public plunderers under the silence of midnight" was the way Calhoun described those responsible for the removal. Clay felt the President had assumed wrongful control of the Treasury and that his reasons for removing the deposits from the Bank were "unsatisfactory and insufficient."

The Bank resorted to reprisals. In six months it reduced its loans by almost $10 million. This was a deliberate attempt to cudgel the President into granting a new charter, but Jackson would not be terrorized by the "hydra of corruption," as he called the Bank. It "is trying to kill me," he told Van Buren, "but I will kill it." Now a financial crash was inevitable. It might have come anyway, but Jackson's gradual removal of deposits from the Bank would have made for a tolerable transition period had Biddle not responded with

restrictive measures on the credit. Factories began to shut down. Philadelphia, which had issued 600 building permits during one period of 1833, issued only eight during the same period in 1834. Grain prices fell sharply. Some companies were forced to postdate paychecks four or five months. Denunciations, petitions and distress memorials poured in upon the President, along with delegations egged on by Biddle and Clay. But Jackson felt that most of the "panic" was artificial, caused by those who "live by borrowing, trade on loans, and gamblers in stocks." In part, he was right. Even John Quincy Adams had the grace to admit that credit abuses and a heedless pursuit of profit were the immediate causes.

For all the petitioners Jackson's answer was the same. "Why am I teased with committees?" he demanded. "Go to Nicholas Biddle. . . . Go to the monster. . . . The people, sir, are with me." They were. The people believed Jackson to be right even when he was wrong. They knew he was fighting their fight. They thrilled to his outburst against what they widely considered to be a subversively rebellious group: "If that be your game," he exclaimed, "come with your armed Bank mercenaries, and, by the Eternal, I will hang you around the Capitol on gallows higher than Haman."

Business pressure finally forced Biddle to retreat. With money again available and credit easy, the second round of the economic cycle was suddenly under way—a wild boom. Land sales doubled and redoubled. Speculation ran rife. "I did not join in putting down the Bank . . . to put up a wilderness of local banks," declared the alarmed "Old Bullion" Benton. Eastern hard-money men agreed. Jackson listened to them. Then, dismayed by the wild issue of paper bank money in the West and excessive speculation in the public lands, he put a stop to it—so drastically that the country plunged from inflation into disaster. On July 11, 1836, he issued the Specie Circular, declaring that deposit banks and receivers of public money could accept nothing but coin for the sale of public lands. Jackson had hoped that this move would halt the ruinous speculation in public lands and curb the inflation rampant in the nation. But while his order was sound in theory, it was destructive in timing and practice. The result was to drain much of the gold in the East westward. There was consternation among Eastern businessmen. Loans were

Editor Amos Kendall masterminded much of Jackson's political strategy. He wrote many of the President's state papers—and also wrote editorials favoring the state papers which he sent to friendly editors around the country. Then he quoted them in his own journal to show the country approved.

This is the Cow.
With the crumpled Horn,
That tossed the Dog, that worried the Cat,
That caught the Rat, that eat the Malt,
That laid in the house that Jack built.

This is the Maiden all forlorn,
That kissed the Maiden all forlorn,
That tossed the Dog, that worried the Cat,
That caught the Rat, that eat the Malt,
That laid in the House that Jack built.

Martin Van Buren

This is the Man all tattered and torn,
That kissed the Maiden all forlorn,
That milked the Cow with the crumpled horn,
That tossed the Dog that worried the Cat,
That caught the Rat, that eat the Malt,
That laid in the House that Jack built.

Fra'L. Blair.

This is the Priest all shaven and shorn,
That married the Man all tattered and torn,
That kissed the Maiden all forlorn,
That milked the Cow with the crumpled Horn,
That tossed the Dog, that worried the Cat,
That caught the Rat, that eat the Malt,
That laid in the House that Jack built.

Attacking Jackson, this waspish Whig cartoon depicts him astride a porker waxing fat on political fare. Jackson did not say "to the victors belong the spoils," and he frowned on dishonest dealings, but his errors in judging men could be spectacular. His New York collector of customs, Samuel Swartwout, became the first American in history to steal a million dollars.

called up. In March 1837 a panic in England brought a further drain on American gold supplies. That spring three great cotton firms failed in New Orleans; 128 companies in New York went under by April. Stocks crashed. In May came a run on the nation's banks and they suspended payment in coin. A hungry mob broke into a New York warehouse, pelted the mayor with flour and threw barrels and sacks from the window, finally destroying an estimated 1,000 bushels of wheat and 500 barrels of flour.

H OWEVER badly executed Jackson's economic policies may have been, no one can deny that they were well intentioned. The same cannot be said —at least by the standards of a later generation—for another of his policies, which affected the Indians of the Southern states and territories. The issue here involved state violations of federal pacts with the Indians; in the most flagrant of these acts the governor of Georgia, in complete defiance of the federal treaties, sent surveyors onto the Indian lands preparatory to handing them over to white settlers.

The President and the courts were charged with enforcing the treaties, but Jackson took no action. And when the Supreme Court later ruled in favor of the Indians, Jackson, displaying his customary highhanded attitude toward the judiciary, is said to have commented: "John Marshall has made his decision; now let him enforce it."

Jackson's stand was in keeping with his character and background. He was first and last a frontiersman, with the frontiersmen's ingrained hostility toward Indians. As a human being he could be kind to them in individual instances. But as a backwoods soldier he had fought and defeated them. As a regional politician, moreover, he had long followed the usual custom of using Indian troubles as a stick with which to beat government authorities into granting military protection and other concessions to the white settlers. Now, as President, he was not going to stand up for the rights of the red man against those of the whites.

It was also true that as late as 1829 the United States had had no more than a token Indian policy. For more than 200 years now, the Indians had conveniently melted away as the whites moved slowly forward. Now the advance was like a flood tide; the Indians were being overrun and were growing increasingly restive, and something had to be done. Years before, Jefferson had dreamed of uniting all the tribes beyond the Mississippi River, far from the reach of the white man. Others had suggested educating them so they could be absorbed into white society.

The young Calhoun, as Monroe's Secretary of War, had viewed the plight of the Indians with pity. He had suggested vocational education—farming and mechanical studies for the boys, spinning and sewing for the girls—plus resettlement as the only sensible solution. Accordingly, Monroe in 1825 laid before Congress a master plan to remove all Eastern tribes to "permanent" sites west of the Mississippi, where it was thought that the white man would never care to go.

Actually, by pressure rather than plan, this kind of migration had been going on all the time. But frontier agitation for legal adoption of the program mounted steadily through the Adams Administration. So when Jackson took office, he introduced the necessary measures with dispatch and relish. In 1830 the Indian Removal Act became the law of the land.

When War Department teams arrived to negotiate new treaties, the Indians received them with a calm born of despair. Since their first sight of the white man, they had been the victims of his guns, his devious politics, his firewater and his diseases. To the Indian mind, land was the gift of the Great Spirit, to be used gratefully. Most tribes lived in a kind of simple communism; the idea of individual land ownership was unknown to them, and the concept of transferring land titles was a mystery that many could not grasp. "I touched the goose quill to the treaty," the chief Black Hawk later said, "not knowing, however, that by that act I consented to give away my village." Many tribes thus unknowingly cooperated in their own undoing.

The Indians of the Northeast presented no real problem. By 1830 they were nothing but a shattered jumble of remnants. The once-powerful Six Nations Iroquois had been smashed by the Revolution; the pro-British majority had fled into Ontario and only a small pro-American element remained in New York State, rewarded for their loyalty with a life of squalor and privation. The Delaware of the Middle Atlantic Coast had been gradually forced to move across the Mississippi River.

Osceola, tribal leader in the second Seminole War, was slender and "good looking, with rather an effeminate smile," but he was a formidable warrior. Treacherously seized by U.S. troops during truce talks, he languished three months in prison. Then, painting half his face vermilion in a traditional oath of war, he died— some thought of a broken heart.

IN the old Northwest, the Indians had rallied briefly under their brilliant leader, Tecumseh. His dream was a mighty one—to end any further cession of Indian lands, and to unite all tribes from the Floridas to the Great Lakes in one mighty confederation. His fire and eloquence almost accomplished this. But his Indians were crushed at Tippecanoe, ending the dream. Tecumseh himself was slain in frontier fighting during the War of 1812.

Early in the century, the Sauk had ceded most of what is now northwestern Illinois, southern Wisconsin and eastern Missouri. Black Hawk, the tribe's foremost chief, later renounced the treaty. The Americans then did business with a more willing Sauk named Keokuk, and negotiated new treaties with him. Black Hawk found his lands overrun by white squatters and his people hounded by troops sent to enforce the cessions. He led his tribe across the Mississippi, but the soldiers followed. When in desperation he sent emissaries to the whites, they were killed. At last Black Hawk fought back—and volunteers promptly poured out of every frontier hamlet to hunt him down. Young Captain Abraham Lincoln, hiking cross-country with a band of "hay foot, straw foot" Illinois irregulars, was spared the ugly sight of others catching up with Black Hawk. For when federal troops trapped the chief's forces, a white flag of surrender was flying. They ignored it and cold-bloodedly shot the Indians down.

Of some 500 braves, with their women and children, only a handful escaped slaughter. Black Hawk surrendered and was brought to Washington as a prisoner. There he came face to face with a battle-scarred warrior who, like himself, was nearing 70: Andrew Jackson. The chief told the President: "I am a man and you are another. I took up the hatchet for my part to avenge injuries which my people could no longer endure. . . . I say no more of it; it is known to you." In 1833 Black Hawk was released, but not before he was paraded as an exhibit through the streets of several Eastern cities. Now, however, the volatile public, instead of looking down on him, lionized the old chief. At last Black Hawk was permitted to join the pitiful remnant of his tribe in Iowa. His last stand, which was dignified by the name of the Black Hawk War, marked the end of Indian resistance in the region.

John Ross, though he had but a trace of Indian blood, was beloved by the Cherokee. He fought with them against the Creeks and rose to become chief. His aristocratic bearing led George Catlin, who drew this portrait, to "testify to the ... urbanity of his manner ... and the purity of his language."

John Jolly, Cherokee chief, adopted young Sam Houston, who ran away from home to be among "the untutored children of the forest." Chief Jolly gave up his lands voluntarily. Other tribesmen were so enraged by this that they pronounced the death penalty on any Indian who followed his example.

It was in the South that the drama of Indian removal was played out to its greatest tragedy. For the Five Civilized Tribes who lived here were well on their way to being absorbed in the mainstream of American life. They had good homes, prosperous farms; many were well-to-do. Many of the Creek and Choctaw natives had intermarried with the whites, had adopted the white man's dress, and lived in the white man's houses. The compact Chickasaw nation, whose braves had never lost a major battle, had developed a new breed of horse. The Cherokee nation had built roads, schools and churches; by 1828 these eager, adaptable people had invented a written language and were printing their own newspaper. In Florida, the Seminole, who had split off from the Creeks, were prospering. Their population, swelled by the remnants of other tribes and runaway Negro slaves, was almost trebled by refugees fleeing the armies of Jackson during the War of 1812.

But once the Indian Removal Act was law, Georgia, Alabama and Mississippi could hardly wait to clear the five great tribes from their fertile lands. To the whites, the only Indian worse than an uncivilized Indian was a civilized (and therefore competitive) one. So, in defiance of treaties the Indians had signed with the federal government, these states proceeded to annex Indian lands. Georgia passed laws abolishing tribal rule and putting the Indians directly under state jurisdiction. While bootleggers kept the tribes demoralized with whiskey, hordes of squatters and speculators invaded the Indian territory, seeking free land.

THEN came the battle before the Supreme Court, led and won for the Indians by the brilliant attorney William Wirt. The court ruled that the states had no right to pass laws contrary to federal treaties with the Indians. But Jackson looked upon Wirt's struggle as "wicked," insisting that he had roused hopes among the Indians that public opinion would never permit to be fulfilled. Jackson could have enforced the decision had he wished, but he wanted the Indians removed, treaties or no treaties.

So Jackson—or "Sharp Knife," as the Indians had called him since the old Creek War days—appealed to the Indians themselves. He journeyed southward and went among the chiefs, urging their "voluntary" removal to Oklahoma. He offered liberal inducements of money and land.

Some agreed to go. Others were forced. Helplessly the braves wandered about, giving farewell touches to beloved rocks and streams. Then, in the bitter cold winter of 1831, the first migrants, small bands of Choctaw, departed. The promised government money did not arrive. Ice floes in the Mississippi and then outbreaks of cholera decimated the tribes. The Creeks were put out on the road in 1836, with their unwilling tribesmen manacled and chained in double file. About 3,500 of this nation's 15,000 would be dead of hunger and exposure by the time they reached Oklahoma. In 1837 the Chickasaw, laden with baggage and slowed by their herds of horses, turned their faces and heavy hearts westward. A year later the 17,000 Cherokee started their migration, 4,000 of them perishing along the way. Ever afterward the Indians would know this enforced journey as "the trail of tears."

The Seminole determined to fight. The result was the longest (seven years) and costliest ($20,000,000 and 1,500 troops killed) of the United States' Indian wars. The Seminole lost their best leader when the bold, elusive young Osceola was seized while parleying under a flag of truce. He died three months later in military prison. Not until August 1842 was a Seminole treaty of peace signed. Then, except for a small group which hid out in the Florida Everglades (and never did officially make peace with the United States), they too were herded westward into Oklahoma.

The woes of the emigrant Indians did not stop on the far side of the Mississippi. They were scourged by epidemics, betrayed or abandoned by the whites for gain or expediency, set upon by warlike Western Indians whose own troubles were just beginning. However, by the time Jackson's hand-picked successor, Martin Van Buren, completed his four-year term, the removal was virtually complete, and a shameful episode in the nation's history was, for the moment, at an end.

IN the summer of 1836 Jackson made a campaign tour in Tennessee for Van Buren. It was too much for the frail hero. After his return to the White House he collapsed, bleeding from the lungs, and was put to bed. For two days it was a question whether he would live or die. From then on, Jackson's greatest task was merely to live. His unyielding will held off this enemy as it had all earlier challengers. His hair grew whiter, his face more deeply lined. He had to give up his long walks and horseback rides. He came downstairs only five times between November 1836 and March 4, 1837.

His last battle was fought out on the floor of the Senate. On January 16, 1837, a committee room in the Capitol could have doubled for the Senate restaurant. It was laden with ham, turkey, beef, pickles, coffee and wines. For here Benton had spread a feast to sustain the "expungers," the loyal Jackson men who would fight that day and night to bring about the last Jacksonian victory, the expunging of the resolution of censure for the removal of deposits. On the day the vote was taken, Clay appeared dressed all in black; it was said he was in mourning for the Constitution. For the censure was expunged, and Jackson was exonerated.

At the inauguration in 1837, the crowd did not gaze at Martin Van Buren but at the frail old man with the bowed head who was near him. "For once," observed Benton, "the rising was eclipsed by the setting sun." When it was all over and Jackson began to descend the steps to his carriage, a great shout rent the air, such "as power never commanded. . . . It was affection, gratitude, and admiration," and Benton felt "an emotion which had never passed through me before."

Van Buren graciously asked the retired Executive to remain for at least a month as his guest at the White House before attempting the journey home. But Jackson would stay only two days. The next day, meeting with friends, Jackson issued a warning: "Never once take your eyes off Texas, and never let go of fifty-four-forty [the Oregon country]." And he voiced a regret that he had not shot Henry Clay or hanged John C. Calhoun.

These remarks show the dualism of the man: his surface impulsiveness, his underlying carefulness where the public safety was concerned. Undoubtedly he would have liked to have been another Jefferson, who doubled the size of the country. But he knew that to bring in Texas would mean war with Mexico and to settle the boundary dispute in Oregon on his terms would mean war with England—and he had pledged peace. On the other hand, he had bluffed France with the promise that he would seize French property if long-outstanding debts were not paid. His violent threat worked. Though France

Menewa, fabled Creek chieftain, was an old adversary of Andrew Jackson. But he later took up the white man's ways, becoming the owner of large herds of cattle. He was even a U.S. ally in the fight against the Seminole. Nevertheless, when the Creeks were exiled, Menewa was exiled with them.

talked of war, in the end a peaceful solution was reached through English mediation. American prestige was never so high. Europe had been forcibly reminded that a treaty with the United States could not be ignored.

Yet the legacy of Jacksonian democracy was mixed. His Indian policies were indefensible. In politics, more significant than the abuses of the spoils system was the increased use of government as a partisan political machine. Economically, the people suffered during Jackson's presidency. In tampering with the currency he had brought crashing down upon the people the very disasters he had hoped to avoid. Though in crushing the Bank he had ended a real threat to democratic processes, in doing so he had had to yield both to the inflationists and the hard-money men. He had opposed both privilege and irresponsible banking, but in warring on one he had released the other.

Out of all this came the most ironic lesson of all: that if a man talks with real sincerity about saving the people, no matter how his actions may hurt them, they will still love him. It was Jackson's dedication that the people sensed. They went right on voting for him—he probably could have been President for a third and fourth and fifth term. Years after his death, men were still voting for Andrew Jackson.

KING ANDREW THE FIRST.

"King Andrew the First" tramples the Constitution in this cartoon by the political opposition. Jackson's repeated flouting of Supreme Court decisions infuriated the Whigs; they referred to him as a dictator, tyrant and demagogue. But it was helpless invective: although the Whigs had the newspapers and cartoonists on their side, Jackson had the voters on his.

HE left Van Buren a legacy of disaster. The Little Magician's troubles began with the election of his running mate, Richard Mentor Johnson, who was the personal selection of Jackson. Voters had separate presidential and vice-presidential choices in those days, and they failed to give Johnson a clear majority. As a consequence the vice-presidential election had to go into the Senate, for the only time in United States history, before Johnson could assume the office.

Panic held the country in its grip. It was the worst depression the United States had ever known, but by the time it struck, Jackson—who bore a heavy responsibility for the crash—had left the White House, as popular as ever. At the height of the 1837 panic Van Buren was President, so it was his problem. All were affected. Britain clamped down on its credit. Cotton prices dropped to catastrophically low levels. Wheat, rye and oats sold at exorbitant prices. In New York mobs gathered at the locked doors of factories. By the summer of 1837, no less than 90 per cent of the Eastern factories had shut down. By winter the destitute filled city streets, and families evicted for nonpayment of rent clung to each other for warmth outside their former homes. Snow fell upon them. Many starved. Many froze.

And Van Buren? The Magician had no rabbits to pull out of his hat. He sat by. Hungry for reassurance, the people would have greeted any encouraging message, but he issued none. The man who could manipulate so brilliantly behind the scenes could not act himself. He preferred to deal with fundamentals, and fundamentals meant little politically.

He had a plan, which was to divorce the banking system permanently from the federal government. He proposed setting up for the government's use a series of subtreasuries in the nation's leading cities as repositories for the federal funds. All money that was due the United States would have to be paid in gold, silver or Treasury notes. This would deal another blow to speculation in the public lands.

The foremost champion of this plan on the floor of Congress was Calhoun, and his return to the Democratic party enraged the Clay Whigs who had looked upon him as their ally. It was Calhoun's influence that finally pushed the subtreasury bill through in 1840.

Calhoun was looking far beyond a mere banking system. In taking his stand he had made what has been called the most significant single decision reached by an American leader before the Civil War. He was looking toward a realignment of the entire American political party system. The businessmen of the North and the planters of the South had long been united in the Whig party. Calhoun's aim now was to draw all Southerners into the ranks of the Democrats, the great plantation owners along with the smaller farmers of the Jeffersonian tradition.

There was a logic here. The Whigs still favored a centralized National Bank; a Bank favored Eastern industrialism; Eastern industrialism, Calhoun saw, would support slavery only so long as it received no economic challenge from it. In the end, therefore, industrialism was the deadly enemy of Southern agrarianism. Hence the South must unite in one party for its own protection and must support a decentralized banking system under which the wealth of the country could not be sucked into central coffers in the East. The South must unite against the "terrible giant" of finance capitalism. Thus were drawn the battle lines of the future.

Meanwhile, lines had formed for a battle of an entirely different kind. One of the more ridiculous election contests in American history got under way in 1840 with a log cabin and cider barrels on display in the principal cities. Mediocrity triumphed; the time for greatness was over. The first President to be really chosen by the people—or rather by the party leaders—was William Henry Harrison, who had been defeated in 1836 by Van Buren. Harrison was still the same man as the candidate who had lost four years before, but his public relations campaign was different. If the people no longer had "Old Hickory," they could now have "Old Tippecanoe," the log-cabin candidate, and a greater American military hero "than any other . . . now living." They could have a "Jackson candidate" who, though he had no policies whatever, Jacksonian or otherwise, was praised because:

> He lives in a cabin built of logs,
> Drinks nothing but hard cider too,
> He plows his own ground, and feeds his own hogs,
> This fellow of Tippecanoe.

Against myths such as these it mattered little that Harrison actually lived in a 16-room mansion on an estate of 3,000 acres. It did not matter that Van Buren, who had been born and reared in grim poverty, was the real "man of the people." Van Buren ate with gold spoons and perfumed his whiskers—these were the "issues" that mattered. The people went to the polls and elected the machine-made recipient of all this shrewd propaganda.

For the first time in the history of the republic, declared the *Washington Globe,* "the power of money has triumphed over intelligence." Jacksonian democracy had come full circle. Jackson had proved the people wanted a military hero; now they had one.

Then fate struck. The elderly President died one month after his inauguration—and his running mate, John Tyler, a former Democrat who had been slipped onto the ticket simply to woo anti-Jacksonian Democratic votes in the South, was, by the grace of God, President of the United States.

The "Log Cabin March" (above) helped end the Jackson era. Whig candidate William Henry Harrison, victor of Tippecanoe, had an issue—"$2 a day and roast beef for everyone"—but mostly he had melodies. He had the "Tippecanoe Waltz" to dance to, the march to march to and thousands of people to sing: "Tippecanoe and Tyler too. And with 'em we'll beat little Van."

Congress and politics in command

D URING the second decade of the 19th Century, a new generation of congressmen rode into office on a wave of nationalism. By 1813, three giant figures who would dominate legislation until 1850 had arrived on the scene. Two (below) were born to be antagonists: John Calhoun of South Carolina, the "cast-iron man" who championed states' rights and slavery, and Daniel Webster of Massachusetts, whose organ voice and impassioned rhetoric often rang out in behalf of mercantile New England. At least their equal was Kentucky's Henry Clay (opposite), beloved even by adversaries. Clay caught the spirit of the age and represented it best as the high priest of compromise.

This new generation lacked the background, intellectual scope and moral grandeur of the founding fathers. Essentially its members were professional politicians, consummately skilled at appealing to—and representing—the ambitions and prejudices of their grass-roots constituents. It was as partisans, with strong provincial and party loyalties, that they grappled with the bewildering new problems created by America's rapid growth and diversification. Yet as hardheaded realists, they managed to reconcile innumerable conflicts of interest into national policy and working law. In so doing, they raised Congress to unprecedented power as the clearinghouse of the democratic process.

"BLACK DAN" WEBSTER in 1830 attacks the Southern states for defying federal law. To defend the South, John Calhoun (far left) resigned as the Vice President and got elected senator.

"GALLANT HARRY" CLAY stands (opposite) among symbols of his great career. Only the presidency, which he pursued as "a Western man . . . with Northern principles," eluded his grasp.

The House in action

The old chamber of the House of Representatives, now Statuary Hall, comes aglow in solemn splendor as the candles of the great chandelier are lit for an evening session in 1822. This picture, a detail of a painting by Samuel F. B. Morse, contains individual portraits of 65 of the 183 members then in the

House plus assorted others—Supreme Court justices (on the dais at left rear), a senator, reporters, a clerk, even a Pawnee Indian chief in the gallery at right. Compared with the Senate, whose members were elected by state legislatures, the House in the 1800s was truly "of the people." The representatives were an earthy lot whose high spirits erupted often—into laughter at the coarse humor of frontier congressmen, into violence on the floor and duels along the Potomac. Many were drinkers. Others gambled, and Henry Clay, elected Speaker six times, was not the only one to lose a fortune at cards.

AMUSING THE HOUSE, back-woods Representative Davy Crockett rouses his fellows with his earthy humor. Made a legend by the press, Davy was said to have bragged he would "eat any man opposed to Jackson." But he later opposed Old Hickory himself.

The influence of the press in political wars

As the battles in Congress increased in bitterness and complexity, the press rose to new heights of power, thriving on the public's growing appetite for political news. Partisan journals kept battalions of writers busy influencing as well as informing their readers.

In the early 1800s a new element was added. Lithography—a cheap, simple method of reproducing pictures from stone—was imported from Europe, and suddenly political handbills blossomed on fences and walls all across the land. Thousands of these pictures, some of them hand-colored, were sold for a dime or a quarter and were hung in living rooms and front windows. Artists with pens dipped in vitriol were enrolled by the lithography companies. In their hands the cartoon became, by the 1830s, a deadly weapon of political warfare.

SILENCING JACKSON, Henry Clay is shown stitching the President's lips during the battle over the Bank of the U.S. The Senate had censured Jackson and he wrathfully replied. Then Clay refused to let Jackson's retort be officially recorded in the Senate.

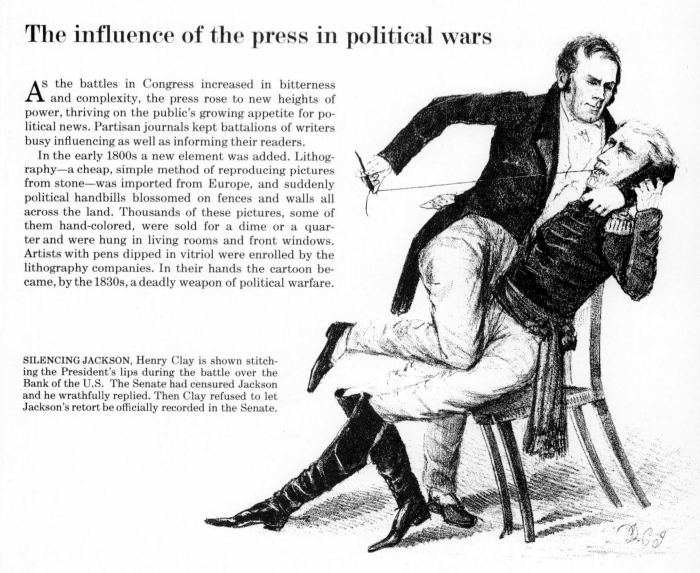

"Sun of Intellectual light & liberty, stand ye still, in Masterly inactivity, that the Nation of Carolina may continue to hold Negroes & plant Cotton till the day of Judgment!"

MOCKING CALHOUN, a lithograph depicts him as "Joshua, Commanding the Sun to Stand Still," imputing to him the reactionary aims inscribed in the balloon above. Fittingly, the sun *(upper left)* which Calhoun seeks to halt is a printing press, the power of which he had ample opportunity to regret during the nullification crisis and in the later struggles over slavery.

THE CAPITOL, center of power, rears its copper-covered dome over the soggy plain of early Washington. The building's north and south wings were begun in 1851, its present iron dome five years later.

THE PEOPLE, the source of power, gather in a carnival mood to vote in Independence Hall. By the mid-1830s, improved roads sped Philadelphia's election returns to Washington in just two days.

Party machines to tap the roots of national power

Exciting new leadership in Congress was but one aspect of the political change sweeping America. Between the elections of 1824 and 1844, the vote for President jumped some 750 per cent, while the population did not quite double. Contributing to this disproportionate increase were the ballots of many citizens formerly disenfranchised by poverty or lack of property. But even greater numbers were simply awakening to the practical consequences of national policy and beginning to vote their personal, business and sectional interests.

As the electorate expanded, techniques for harnessing its power grew more sophisticated. The political parties reached out from the U.S. Capitol into every ward, for as Andrew Jackson put it, "To give effect to any principles, you must avail yourself of the physical force of an organized body of men. . . ." Marshaled by efficient local machines, voters came out with a gusto *(below)* that appalled those who feared the rule of "King Mob."

A great burst
of oratory
that ended an age

The slavery issue, which had flared up repeatedly in Congress, erupted once again when California asked to join the Union as a free state in 1849. Like an old firehorse answering the alarm, Henry Clay arrived, re-elected senator following seven years' absence. Now 72 and infirm, "The Great Pacificator" had to be helped up the Senate steps on February 5, 1850, but his old power returned as he started to set forth (right) a "comprehensive scheme of settling amicably the whole question in all of its bearings."

Clay's Compromise of 1850 was mercilessly attacked by Calhoun (standing third from right) and brilliantly defended by Webster (seated at left with cupped ear). Debate raged on into summer. Finally in September the plan was rammed through as five separate laws. It would preserve the Union for 10 years more. But it marked the last important appearance of the three giants and signaled the end of a splendid age.

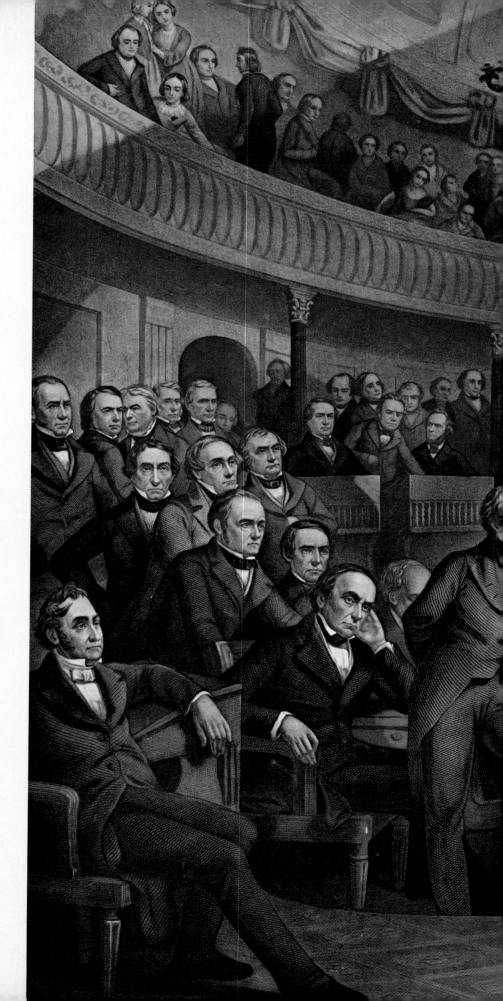

3. THE PURSUIT OF PERFECTION

IN the mixed farming, forest and manufacturing country of western Pennsylvania in the 1840s an oasis of tranquil green glowed on a plain above the waters of the Ohio River. Its well-kept fences and rich fields rippling in the summer breezes were in sparkling contrast to the more modest farmland and tangled woods surrounding it. This was the settlement of the Harmony Society, one of numerous "communistic" groups which existed in the industrial and intellectual ferment of 19th Century America. Inspirationists, Shakers, Perfectionists, Mormons—all across the country a great array of hopeful Utopians established communities, each avowedly communistic in its pooling of resources and earnings for the good of all.

This was not, of course, Communism as later generations would know it. The militant international movement of Marx and Engels, with its emphasis on class war and revolution, did not yet exist. The American communists of the early and middle 1800s were peaceful people seeking a better way to live by sharing the profits of their toil with their neighbors.

The communistic societies were only one part of a vast search for perfection that obsessed Americans of the 1840s. Any man, the American philosopher Ralph Waldo Emerson wrote to the British historian Thomas Carlyle, might have a plan for a model society in his pocket. This intellectual turmoil had its beginnings in the 1830s, as Americans started to read more and more. There was the penny press, epitomized by the New York *Herald* and the New York

AN ADROIT POLITICIAN, Martin Van Buren wears a satisfied expression in this portrait—but as Jackson's handpicked successor he reaped problems his patron sowed.

Sun. Magazines like *Godey's Lady's Book, The Knickerbocker* and the *Southern Literary Messenger* were circulated widely. The South Carolinian William Gilmore Simms was writing his robust tales of the Yamassee War. Edgar Allan Poe, lost in an alcoholic maze, was sharing his nightmare world with horrified and fascinated readers.

The first volume of George Bancroft's *History of the United States* had appeared by 1834, as well as Davy Crockett's heavily embroidered *Autobiography*. Washington Irving was writing of his travels in Spain and the American West. James Fenimore Cooper was creating romantic characters such as Leatherstocking, Chingachgook and Uncas in his tales of noble forest savages.

In Boston, the little essayist-poet Dr. Oliver Wendell Holmes was preening himself on his status as first citizen of "the Hub of the Universe." But also in Massachusetts, Nathaniel Hawthorne was pondering the question of evil in *The Scarlet Letter*, which he started to write in 1849, while all the powers of darkness seemed to be hovering over Herman Melville as he wrote *Pierre* and *Moby Dick*, novels "broiled in hell-fire." It was no accident perhaps that so much intellectual fire came out of New England, with its Protestant tradition, its harsh winters and its tight little farms girded with rocks and loneliness.

Reform was surging up along with the creativity. Emerson, the philosopher and essayist, described a motley group that had gathered in Boston to protest and to pray as "madmen, madwomen, men with beards, Dunkers, Muggletonians, Come-outers, Groaners, Agrarians, Seventh-Day Baptists, Quakers, Abolitionists, Calvinists, Unitarians, and Philosophers." But there was room for each and all.

One ardent Utopian called 1843 "the wonderful year." That year a Vermont constable, William Miller, declared the world was about to end, and all over New England and New York Millerites made their ascension robes, chalked "Prepare to meet your God" on boulders and mounted roofs to await their ascent to the hereafter. Others concentrated their hopes on this world. In Illi-

LEADERS IN AN EMERGING LITERARY TRADITION

Novelist James Fenimore Cooper loved the wilderness. From Europe in 1831 he spoke of his yearning "to plunge into the forests." But returning, he found a land that was growing more and more urbanized, and raged: "God protect the country that has nothing but commercial towns for capitals."

Nathaniel Hawthorne stood aside from his times, but he had strong opinions. He condemned use of the nude figure in art, and he thought the frank views on sex expressed by Margaret Fuller (opposite page) were improper, for they furnished clues by which her mind's "inmost secrets may be searched out."

Herman Melville led an adventurous life, even visiting the South Sea cannibals—although his father had considered him so frail he advised the boy to "avoid green fruit and unseasonable exposure to the sun." In another wrong guess, the father represented his son as "slow in comprehension."

William Gilmore Simms was the South's leading novelist and also a prolific writer of history, biography and poetry. His publisher said he could write more in a half hour than a printer could set in a week. Poe called him "the best writer of fiction in America"— but the South all but ignored him.

nois, Joseph Smith was receiving divine revelations regarding the sanctity of polygamy and was eagerly passing them on to his Latter-day Saints, otherwise known as Mormons. Elsewhere in the country, the advocates of women's rights, of total abstinence from alcohol and of sundry other uplifting causes were preaching their doctrines.

The most publicized of America's variegated 19th Century communistic groups was Brook Farm, the grand experiment of the Transcendental movement. New England's Transcendentalists sought to transcend human experience, to seek a higher spiritual reality. The underlying logic of their rationale lay in Unitarianism, which swept like a scythe across New England early in the 19th Century, cutting down the old Puritan dogmas, preaching the oneness of God, the goodness of man and the sacredness of reason, insisting that human problems were capable only of human solution. However, while the Transcendentalists accepted the Unitarian doctrine that Christ was not God (but had honored man by becoming man), they went even further. They saw the individual soul as a part of God—so man's ultimate self-reliance was not to be questioned.

At Brook Farm, the Transcendentalists put this self-reliance to the test. "Our ulterior aim is nothing less than Heaven on Earth," the newspaper editor Charles A. Dana declared. The 200-acre colony, nine miles from Boston, was founded by George Ripley, who had been a Unitarian minister. Its immediate goal was, in his words, "to insure a more natural union between intellectual and manual labor."

Unfortunately, the Transcendentalist group was not very well organized to achieve this lofty aim. It should have had a far higher percentage of manual laborers and a much lower percentage of intellectuals than it actually had. Even so, the place was an earthly paradise for a time. "There were never such witty potato-patches and such sparkling cornfields," one member recalled later. Boston was handy for intellectual refreshment, and most of those who

WARRIORS FOR THE RIGHTS OF WOMEN

Emma Hart Willard, founder of the Troy Female Seminary, at first could not afford to hire professors to teach science subjects. So she studied up and taught them herself. She also wrote poetry, but the only verses that survive are the lyrics to that basso's despair, "Rocked in the Cradle of the Deep."

Dorothea Dix, who battled to improve the lot of the insane, stood for no nonsense. A pupil recalled that as a schoolteacher "it was in her nature to use the whip, and use it she did." Later as superintendent of nurses in the Civil War her rule was brief: "All nurses are required to be plain-looking."

Frances Wright, crusader for the rights of American women, was born in Scotland. She visited the United States when she was 23 and again when she was 29, and finally decided to stay and change things. She was against religion, legal marriage and banks, and in favor of emancipating the slaves.

The free woman's ideal was Margaret Fuller. Ralph Waldo Emerson said her genius "obscured her homeliness," but Horace Greeley commented that "a good husband and two or three bouncing babies would have emancipated her from a good deal of cant and nonsense." She later had a son.

shared in the great experiment looked back upon it afterward with pleasure.

Despite a steady turnover in membership, Brook Farm continued from 1841 to 1847—but it had more renown than influence. It produced few great names that were not great already. In fact, the foremost exponents of the Transcendental faith never really settled there. The noted Transcendental teacher Bronson Alcott set up his own ideal society for the contemplation of higher things at Fruitlands, near the village of Harvard, 30 miles west of Boston, but in a bleak January when the money and the members ran out, his "happy dream" became as blighted as winter apples.

By the time the noble experiment ended, Brook Farm was heavily in debt, and the property had to be sold to meet the bills. As for the Transcendentalists' ideas, they caused few lasting ripples. Hawthorne, who had put his scant savings into the community and lived there intermittently for a year, called Brook Farm "certainly the most romantic episode" in his life—"essentially a daydream, and yet a fact." In 1852 he gave the experiment an enduring (and endearing) portrayal in his novel *The Blithedale Romance*. But even Hawthorne believed that "the yeoman and the scholar . . . are two distinct individuals and can never be melted into one substance."

As for the complete Transcendentalist Henry Thoreau, he formed the perfect state (population: one) on the shores of Walden Pond in Concord, where he lived in happy isolation for 26 months. He declined to pay taxes to a national state that permitted slavery—and if this meant doing without the post office, he said, that suited him, for he could think of little news that he cared to receive from the post office anyhow. His desire was to spend his days as deliberately and as silently as nature, and he did. He hoed beans and watched the changing colors of the pond, absorbing nature until, he said, "the whole body is one sense and imbibes delight through every pore."

One leading philosopher of perfection was the French socialist Charles Fourier, whose beliefs—notably that people should be allowed to do whatever work they found themselves best suited for—were officially adopted some years after his death by several American groups that had heard of him from afar, including the Brook Farm communists. Another leading Fourier group was organized at Red Bank, New Jersey. Its members tried to blend farming with small industry; it too had a relatively short life.

The Fourier groups were viewed with tolerance by most Americans, but a great clamor arose against other sects which were thought to challenge the moral values of society. The Mormon leader Joseph Smith was lynched in Illinois in 1844, and his successor as prophet, Brigham Young, was forced to flee with his flock in 1846 to the wilderness of Utah when society refused to accept polygamy as God's plan. A rugged Dartmouth graduate named John Humphrey Noyes, who announced in the 1830s that he had reached the state of sinless perfection, was run out of Putney, Vermont, in 1848, when he extended his belief in the common sharing of all property to include wives. His group of Perfectionists followed him to Oneida, New York.

In Oneida the Perfectionists went on their way happily, and almost undisturbed, for 30 years. Among this group any exclusive attachment of two people for each other was denounced as "selfish love" and condemned. Monogamy and marriage in the conventional sense were forbidden. Children were the children of all. They were taken from their mothers as soon as they were

The Shakers danced their religious services. They formed in two lines, forearms out and hands hanging, then they moved in rhythm toward and away from one another. As they danced they sang religious songs. One was a hymn which went: "With ev'ry gift I will unite, And join in sweet devotion To worship God is my delight, With hands and feet in motion."

weaned and were systematically reared in communal nurseries. One visitor to Oneida expressed concern over these plump and healthy children, with their strange lack of buoyancy and gladness. Yet another observer, admiring them in their beautiful playrooms, thought them an unusually "merry set of infants." And the record shows that these healthy children of eugenic experiment turned out well.

By 1879 there was mounting criticism of the Perfectionists' peculiarities both in New York State and in the Oneida group itself. Noyes, threatened by legal action for his views on marriage and other matters, put himself beyond the reach of the courts by moving across the border to Canada. From that haven he sent back to the community a plan—which was swiftly adopted— permitting the members to marry legally among themselves. In 1880 Oneida was reorganized as a business corporation. In this manifestation, the Oneida Community still thrives and its products—notably its own brand of silver plate—are widely known.

The communistic societies which flourished seem to have been the ones that were not composed primarily of idealistic intellectuals. The "educated people" often quarreled and split up. Generally it was the farmers and workmen, with just a scattering of college graduates and with a strong religious motivation, who made a success of such groups as the Shakers and Perfectionists. The other communistic societies were usually of German origin, and a keen observer noted that "the Germans make better communists than any other people." Whatever their origin, all of these groups lived under a basic communist philosophy, perhaps best voiced by the founders of a later society, the Cedar Vale Community in Kansas: "To achieve both communism and individual freedom, or to lead persons of all kinds of opinions to labor together for their common welfare." In many of these communities all money brought in was turned over to a common fund. Typical of the economic structure were the Aurora Commune in Oregon and Bethel Commune in Missouri, where each family received pigs for meat, cows for milk and land for a vegetable garden, but was also expected to use these benefits to raise a surplus of chickens, eggs and produce which could be traded for other supplies or sold for the good of the community.

IN all groups the individual will was subordinated to the general welfare. Despite a certain elementary form of political democracy, individualism was held in check by the unquestioning obedience given to what the Shakers quaintly called the "leading characters," people like the tall, stoop-shouldered Albert Brisbane, prophet of the Fourierists in America; George Rapp, the kindly founder of the Harmony Society in Pennsylvania; the Mormon leaders Smith and Young; Noyes of the Perfectionists. The Shakers, who by the 1840s were the largest communistic society in America, with 18 settlements from Maine to Kentucky, were guided by the overwhelming spiritual influence of one woman, their hallowed "Mother Ann." A former cook in a Manchester, England, infirmary, who could neither read nor write, she had suffered persecution and lain in jail for her religion, but she was never embittered. "God is love," she said, "and if you love God, you will love one another."

Almost all these societies had some kind of religious basis. The Perfectionists of Oneida believed that community of goods and persons was commanded by Jesus, who would then save all from sin and death. The Mormons

Standing amid the wastes of the Great Salt Valley, Brigham Young and the Mormon elders talk with a chief of the Utes. Although their leaders called this the Promised Land, many a Saint viewed the dismal site of the future bustling Salt Lake City with unmixed dismay. "Weak and weary as I am," moaned one newcomer, "I would rather go a thousand miles farther."

believed that God had especially favored them with a revelation of divine truth. The Separatists, a German group in Zoar, Ohio, lived by a code similar to that practiced by such modern sects as the River Brethren and Mennonites. "All ceremonies are banished from among us," they declared. "We cannot send our children into the schools of Babylon. . . . We cannot serve the state as soldiers."

The strange paroxysms with which the Shakers met representatives of "the spirit world"—the marching, shuffling and whirling, "back and forth as swiftly as if driven by the wind"—excited the greatest curiosity from outsiders. The Shakers believed in celibacy. As a consequence, there were no Shaker offspring to carry on the movement, and it ultimately dwindled. The Harmony Society also was celibate. The watchword of the Inspirationists of the Amana Community, which still flourishes in a much-modified form in Iowa, was: "Fly from intercourse with women, as a highly dangerous magnet and magical fire." But despite efforts to keep the sexes apart, the young man of Amana generally was allowed to marry the girl of his choice. In the Aurora and Bethel communities normal family life was maintained.

IN addition to the Utopian groups, the era saw the beginnings of a feminist movement and the emergence of many remarkable women. Perhaps the most remarkable of them all was Margaret Fuller, editor of the Transcendentalist organ, *The Dial*. Her father started drilling her in Latin when she was six, and in maturity she told her close friend Emerson: "I now know all the people worth knowing in America, and I find no intellect comparable to my own." Despite its arrogance, her statement may have been right; certainly Boston's leading thinkers accepted her as an equal. In 1845 she foreshadowed the whole movement for women's rights with her resounding book, *Woman in the Nineteenth Century*.

She was the first American woman to join the working press, writing effectively for Horace Greeley's New York *Tribune*. "We would have every path laid open to Woman as freely as to Man," she proclaimed, adding: "Let them be sea-captains, if you will." She practiced what she preached to the extent of becoming, if not a sea captain, America's first woman foreign correspondent. She covered the 1848-1849 revolution in Italy and sent the *Tribune* vivid war dispatches. As homely as she was brilliant, she still enjoyed a most romantic career. She married one of the fighters in the Italian revolutionary movement, a handsome Italian marquis, Angelo Ossoli, who was 10 years her junior. But her idyll had a tragic conclusion. In 1850 as she returned to America with her husband and infant son to publish a book on the Italian struggle, the ship was wrecked off the New York coast and all three died. But the noble dreams of her undaunted pioneering were fulfilled by others.

Contrary to a wide popular belief, the early women's rights movement was not the product of fanatics or of frustrated old maids. The first leaders were often wives and mothers like the warmly humorous and intelligent Elizabeth Cady Stanton, who had seven children and simply thought women should share the rights of men as citizens—especially in regard to the vote and the holding of property. The daughter of a lawyer, Mrs. Stanton as a small girl had often heard women helplessly consulting her father about inequities supported by existing law. Wives could own no property and could not share the guardianship of their children. If they worked, their husbands could seize

Elizabeth Cady Stanton, leader in the drive for women's rights, sometimes grew tired of the demands made on her time. Then she would threaten: "As soon as you all begin to ask too much of me, I shall have a baby." And she had seven.

Lucretia Mott, mild, imperturbable Quaker, was Elizabeth Stanton's helper, and a dangerous foe in a debate. Her proud husband was generous with tips to her opponents: "If she thinks thee is wrong, thee had better look it over again."

Martha Wright, Lucretia's sister, kept knitting at a women's rights convention, as did other delegates. When Elizabeth Stanton objected, Martha's daughter advised her in a poem not to get in a "snit/ Against your sisterhood who knit."

their wages. Wife-beating was legal in almost every state; divorce was unusual. For years, Mrs. Stanton fought to get a married woman's property bill enacted in New York State, finally succeeding in 1848.

Meanwhile she had met Lucretia Coffin Mott, a plain-speaking Quaker reformer who had six children, and in July 1848 they organized a women's rights convention at Seneca Falls, New York. As her keynote address, Mrs. Stanton read a "Declaration of Sentiments," an eloquent citation of 18 grievances and wrongs women were suffering from men, "having in direct object the establishment of an absolute tyranny over her." The sequence was similar to the list of charges drawn up against British tyranny in the Declaration of Independence—with "man" cast in the role of George III. Mrs. Stanton also proposed a resolution for women's suffrage, to which the startled Mrs. Mott objected: "Why, Lizzie, thee will make us ridiculous." But Mrs. Stanton insisted that the vote was the key to all women's rights, and the resolution was duly passed.

The women fighting for the ballot were indeed ridiculed and jeered at. *Harper's* magazine called the mere thought of their voting "opposed to nature . . . opposed to revelation." Their struggle was also pitifully handicapped by lack of money. But the movement could neither be stilled nor abandoned; it was riding an irresistible current.

Amelia Jenks Bloomer attended the Seneca Falls meeting, and the next January founded a publication called the *Lily*, crowding it with lively pieces exposing unjust marriage laws and espousing women's right to higher education and the vote. Mrs. Bloomer became the first American woman to be named a deputy postmaster, but what boomed the circulation of the *Lily* and brought her lasting notoriety were her views on dress reform—the tight bodice, short skirt and full trousers soon known as "bloomers." She wore this garb for a number of years, drawing large crowds wherever she talked, and shocked attention wherever she walked. Susan B. Anthony, another notable feminist crusader, tried these Turkish-style trousers too, but gave them up after a year. "I found it a physical comfort but a mental crucifixion," she said. "The attention of my audience was fixed upon my clothes instead of my words. I learned the lesson then that to be successful a person must attempt but one reform."

THE Grimké sisters, Sarah and Angelina, of a conservative and aristocratic family in Charleston, South Carolina, developed an increasing hatred of slavery, and in the 1820s they left home and settled in Philadelphia. The poet Whittier praised them as "Carolina's high-souled daughters," and they became popular public speakers on both abolition and women's rights. In her 1838 *Letters on the Equality of the Sexes and the Condition of Women*, Sarah Grimké stated: "The page of history teems with woman's wrongs. . . . It is wet with woman's tears," and she told women that they were meant to be men's "companions, equals and helpers in every good word and work." Lucy Stone was even more militant—just after she graduated from Oberlin in 1847 she launched into fiery public speaking on the rights and wrongs of her sex, and in 1850 she organized the first national women's rights convention, at Worcester, Massachusetts. When she married Henry Brown Blackwell, she took the title "Mrs." but insisted on keeping her maiden name.

Well aware that the literate citizen was the potent citizen, women put

EXCERPTS FROM THE WOMEN'S "DECLARATION OF SENTIMENTS"

• We hold these truths to be self-evident: that all men and women are created equal.

• The history of mankind is a history of repeated injuries and usurpations on the part of man toward woman, having in direct object the establishment of an absolute tyranny over her.

• He has never permitted her to exercise her inalienable right to the elective franchise.

• He has compelled her to submit to laws, in the formation of which she had no voice.

• He has withheld from her rights which are given to the most ignorant and degraded men—both natives and foreigners.

• He has made her, if married, in the eye of the law, civilly dead.

• He has taken from her all right in property, even to the wages she earns.

• He has denied her the facilities for obtaining a thorough education, all colleges being closed against her.

• He has usurped the prerogative of Jehovah himself, claiming it as his right to assign for her a sphere of action, when that belongs to her conscience and to her God.

• He has endeavored, in every way that he could, to destroy her confidence in her own powers, to lessen her self-respect, and to make her willing to lead a dependent and abject life.

• Now, in view of this entire disfranchisement of one-half the people of this country, we insist that they have immediate admission to all the rights and privileges which belong to them as citizens of the United States.

Horace Mann, who agitated for better schools and better teachers, was a firm believer in phrenology, the "science" of judging character by the shape of the skull, and he also thought that smoking and ballet dancing were harmful. Mann succeeded to the constituency of John Quincy Adams in the House.

A pioneering college for women, Mount Holyoke was founded with $27,000 collected by the indefatigable educator Mary Lyon from no fewer than 1,800 people in 90 towns. She ran it by Spartan rules. The girls could sleep as long as they liked on Thanksgiving— provided they got to breakfast at 8.

education high on their list of demands. In the early 1800s, no college would accept women. The long battle for free public schools, led mainly by educator Horace Mann of Massachusetts was, of course, a benefit to women. But they strove to found their own institutions of higher learning. By the 1820s a valiant schoolteacher, Emma Willard, had established a female seminary in Troy, New York, offering secondary courses in mathematics and science similar to those at boys' schools. The first college-level institution for women was the Mount Holyoke Female Seminary, which Mary Lyon opened in South Hadley, Massachusetts, in 1837.

Temperance was another appealing cause for women, beset as many of them were with sodden and often brutish husbands against whom they had little legal recourse. In America, drinking was a time-honored, if not an inalienable, right. But prison surveys showed a shocking correlation between liquor and crime; it was widely believed, furthermore, that alcohol caused insanity and, worse yet, made the body combustible and likely to burst into flame. All these evils were to be abolished by banning alcohol.

In the area of prison reform and care of the insane, the dedicated Dorothea Lynde Dix was outstanding. America had only eight insane asylums in 1840, and conditions in them were frightful. On March 28, 1841, Miss Dix chanced to be a substitute Sunday-school teacher in a Massachusetts prison. She was appalled to find that part of her class consisted of insane inmates. She had not realized that the custom was to keep the mentally ill behind bars like dangerous beasts. In a campaign that lasted for years Miss Dix succeeded in greatly improving the care of the insane, not only in the United States but also in Europe.

Few reforms were achieved in laboring conditions, whose most pitiful victims were often children and recent immigrants, though some gains were accomplished by the fledgling labor unions and by occasional social reformers like the impassioned Orestes Brownson. The 10-hour day, which was being pressed from the 1830s on, was agreed to by some individual employers; the first state to pass a 10-hour law was New Hampshire in 1847. Even after that, employers found loopholes, notably through special contract clauses that "permitted" the laborer the right to work longer if he wanted to do so. Horace Greeley pointed out the hypocrisy of this in the *Tribune* in 1847, noting that it was "egregious flummery" to talk of freedom of labor when a workman was warned: "If you will work 13 hours per day, or as many as we think fit, you can stay; if not you can have your walking papers: and . . . no one else hereabout will hire you."

THE Constitution would never have been adopted in the first place without the promise of a Bill of Rights. But at the time of its 50th anniversary in 1841, the Bill of Rights was a somewhat shaky bulwark. Its promise of freedom of religion was being challenged by anti-Catholic riots and by "Native American" groups aimed especially at Irish-Americans. Abolitionists and advocates of women's rights were often harassed instead of being granted freedom of speech.

But one of the greatest assaults on the Bill of Rights came from the floor of Congress itself. In 1836, terrified by the potential effect of abolitionist propaganda on Americans, the proslavery faction got through a so-called "gag rule" in the House, restricting the right of petition by barring debate on any slavery petition submitted. In thus trying to cripple the right of petition, guaranteed by the First Amendment, the South probably made more abolitionists in a year than would otherwise have been created in 25. Furthermore, the rule roused the hackles of a powerful opponent—former President John Quincy Adams.

Adams was then nearing 70. But he had effectually solved the problem of what to do with an ex-President. He yielded to the pleas of the voters of the Plymouth District of Massachusetts that he represent them in the House, on condition that he be permitted to do as he deemed right. On these terms he was elected and remained in Congress for almost 17 years.

The doughty congressman from Massachusetts made the repeal of the gag rule his special cause. His main tactic was a simple one: he appointed himself an agent for petitions from all over the country. Day after day, year after year, the hot-tempered old man ("fierce as ten furies, terrible as hell," Representative Andrew Johnson once called him) would bring in new petitions, introduce them in the House and throw the chamber into an uproar. In Adams' view, the Southerners had equated the right of petition with the wrong of slavery—and if slavery could be safeguarded only by denying the right of free speech then indeed it was a threat to all free men.

Suddenly the old Puritan found himself a champion of the people, at least in the North. He had never been a popular figure: character, conscience, conviction he had, but not an atom of charm. He knew little about friendship and suspected treachery on every hand. Yet in his 70s, he who had once been so aloof was kissed by pretty girls and feted in torchlight processions.

But it was not adulation he was after, only justice. His search for perfection caused him to fight tirelessly until the gag rule was rescinded in 1844. The "Old Man Eloquent," born eight years before the shots sounded at Lexington, was cherished now—and not only in the North—as one of the last links with the founding fathers and the Revolution. When he returned to the House after a stroke in 1847, the entire body stood in tribute.

On February 21, 1848, the 80-year-old congressman rose and clutched the side of his desk, as if about to speak. His face was very red. Suddenly he toppled over and was carried to a sofa in the Speaker's office. Henry Clay held his hand, his eyes filling with tears. Once Adams spoke: "This is the end of earth, but I am composed." At the funeral services in Washington, one representative from every state was in attendance. His body was taken to Faneuil Hall in Boston, and over the door of the historic building were the words: "Born a citizen of Massachusetts. Died a citizen of the United States." He was buried in Quincy. At the graveside a Southern congressman leaned over the coffin. "Good-bye, Old Man," he said.

The death of John Quincy Adams, who collapsed in Congress, is seen in a lithograph by Nathaniel Currier (who later formed a famous partnership with James M. Ives). Below is the last note in Adams' hand in the journal he had kept for 66 years; for two years longer, unable to write, he dictated entries.

Quincy Tuesday 30. September 1845.
30. IV.30. Tuesday.
From this time the total disability to write with my own hand compels me to ... the daily journal of my life. I took the Pills prescribed by Dr. Woodward last evening before going to

An era seen by "the eye of history"

HISTORY has been recorded by word of mouth, depicted on the walls of caves, notched on trees, carved on buildings. After 1839, through a magic combination of sunlight, chemicals and optical glass, there came a brilliant new technique for chronicling great events and great men. It showed things not as they looked to a painter but as they really were. It let people stare into the ravaged face and tragic eyes of the poet Edgar Allan Poe *(opposite)*, a few days after he had attempted suicide in the final mad months of his life, and made it possible for them to share a little of his suffering.

This was photography, developed by a handful of Europeans and brought to perfection by Americans. Samuel F. B. Morse, a painter and inventor of the telegraph, was in Paris in 1839 and saw the pictures, luminous on highly polished silver, that Louis Jacques Mandé Daguerre was making. They were called daguerreotypes, and Morse considered them "Rembrandt perfected." He hurried home and began training America's first important professional photographers: Edward B. Anthony, who would be the photographer of Washington's political figures; Albert Southworth, Boston portraitist; and Mathew B. Brady, the future documenter of the Civil War, who saw sharply the real importance of photography. "The camera," said Brady, "is the eye of history."

A PHOTOGRAPHER'S GALLERY is the plush establishment of Jeremiah Gurney, a New York jeweler turned cameraman, in the 1840s. Gurney got his first camera in exchange for a watch.

A MELANCHOLY GENIUS, Edgar Allan Poe sits for a picture that he gave to Mrs. Sarah Whitman, a friend. She said it showed his life's "sullen shadows . . . but it was very fine."

FIREBRAND AUTHOR Harriet Beecher Stowe was daguerreo-
typed by Albert Southworth and his partner Josiah J. Hawes in
the 1850s, soon after her novel, *Uncle Tom's Cabin*, stirred the
North against slavery. Her photographers, by getting rid of
iron headrests, cotton wadding in sagging cheeks and other
trickery, became known for the naturalness of their portraits.

ABOLITIONIST William Lloyd Garrison's daguerreotype of the 1850s showed the flaming spirit of this foe of slavery.

POET Henry Wadsworth Longfellow named "Hiawatha's" heroine from a picture of Minnehaha Falls, Minnesota.

INVENTOR Samuel F. B. Morse, America's first photographer, also shot the first class reunion picture—Yale '10 in 1840.

The famous faces of America

ONE of the camera's most exciting feats was to record forever the features of the nation's notables. Poets and politicians, artists and inventors, all the great personalities of the period sat for their portraits. Pouty old John Quincy Adams posed for daguerreotypes wherever he went; scores of Adams' photographs exist. Andrew Jackson climbed out of his deathbed to be photographed, enduring the ordeal with the stoicism of an old soldier (*next page*). Soon new chemicals—"quicks," they were called—would cut exposure time to 30 seconds, but in the earliest days the camera's subjects had to sit in blazing sunlight without moving for up to 30 minutes. Many distinguished faces were sunburned.

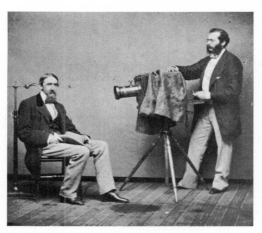

Rigid and uncomfortable, a client sits for a portrait.

STORYTELLER Washington Irving gave this picture to artists who portrayed him, so all their paintings look like it.

HISTORIAN Francis Parkman had sensitive eyes unable to stand sunlight. But he risked them for the camera.

ESSAYIST Ralph Waldo Emerson marveled at the camera: "The artist stands aside and lets you paint yourself."

OLD WARRIOR Andrew Jackson, fatally ill but vigorous of mind and an ardent reader of the political newspapers, was propped up for an unforgettable picture in 1845.

WILY POLITICIAN Martin Van Buren was photographed in 1848, probably by Anthony, when he staged his last campaign for the presidency as the Free-Soil candidate.

EBULLIENT LAWMAKER Thomas Hart Benton turned his Senate committee room over to Anthony to make portraits of famous legislators—including, of course, Benton.

AGING ORATOR Daniel Webster had several daguerreotypes made, and a portrait was painted from one of them. But no painting ever captured the senator as the daguerreotypes did.

ELDER STATESMAN John Quincy Adams criticized most of his daguerreotypes. Nevertheless, this one bore out his own view of himself as "reserved, cold, austere and forbidding."

Cincinnati, with over 60 steamboats tied up along the riverfront, drowses of a September Sunday in 1848. Historians a century later

Portrait of a slumbering city

Ten years after photography was invented, no large city in America was without its portrait studio. Daguerreotype wagons rolled over dusty roads into the back country, daguerreotype flatboats floated down the rivers and Americans had their pictures taken at the rate of three million faces per year. Us-

In a close-up of part of the scene above, three side-wheelers lie moored at the foot of Ludlow Street. The eight panels (this is third from the

figured out the year by the names of the boats, the month by the low level of the river, the day of the week by the peaceful look of the docks.

ing special prisms and mirrors to turn the image around (because the daguerreotype camera produced a backward, or mirror, image), the early cameramen began to make charming pictures of the cities. Few views of New York survive, although that city had the most daguerreotypists, while San Francisco, with fewer photographers, was heavily pictured—the Gold Rush was on and everyone wanted to see the fabulous land. But Cincinnati sat for the most famous picture of an American city in the 1840s—actually eight separate photographs that, when combined, formed the widest-angle panorama of its time.

left) were made by daguerreotypists Charles Fontayne and William Southgate Porter, who set up cameras across the river in Kentucky.

A gallery of Americans proud of their work

From the beginning of time, man had tried to create a record of himself at work; with the arrival of photography this could be done exactly and abundantly. The government hired daguerreotypists to record its doings. Stores and factories were photographed. Men brought the tools of their trade to the galleries. As the price of daguerreotypes—originally at five dollars for a $2\frac{3}{4}$- by $3\frac{1}{4}$-inch silver plate enclosed in its elegant case—sank to $2.50 and then to 50 cents, the flood of photos of men at work increased. Photographers found yet another source of income. Special daguerreotypes showing famous men at work, or re-creating historic events like the one below, were sold in frames for as much as $25.

Firemen, probably of New York, pose in parade uniforms.

A Worcester, Massachusetts, marshal searches a prisoner.

LUNCH HOUR at the woodpile was snapped in 1854 by George Barnard of Syracuse, New York, later one of the Civil War photographers. It shows a worker and his small son resting during a midday break. Barnard entitled this "The Woodsawyer's Nooning."

A HISTORIC MOMENT is recreated as an actor, impersonating the dentist W.T.G. Morton, shows surgeons how to save their patients pain by using ether anesthesia. The picture was made nearly four years after the real demonstration on October 16, 1846.

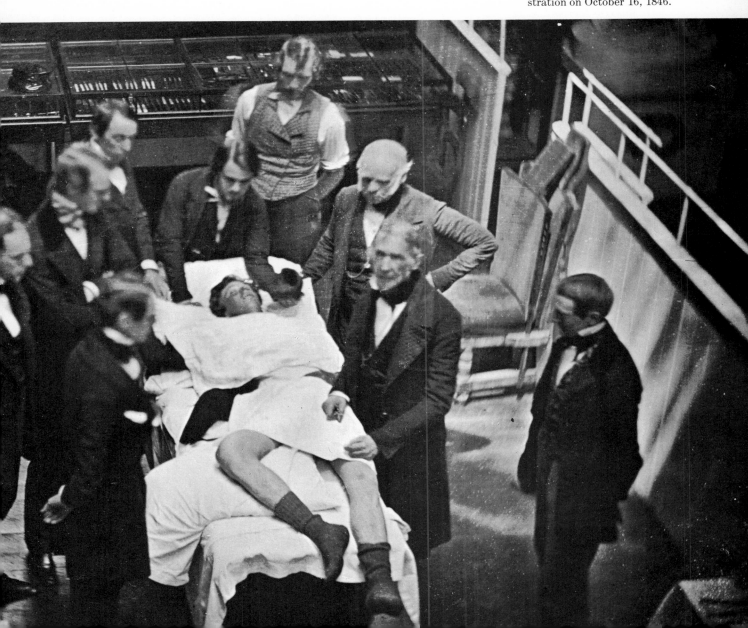

A TRAIN WRECK near Pawtucket, Rhode Island, in 1853 makes history by making the newspaper. A wood engraving of this daguerreotype was published in the New York *Illustrated News*.

Stories of catastrophe told in the blink of a shutter

PICTURES of current events attracted photographers from the moment Daguerre's invention swept the world. Daguerreotypists followed troops of all nationalities into battle everywhere: the Americans into Mexico in 1846, the Russians into Romania in 1853, the British into the Crimea in 1855. They turned up at train wrecks and fires and, as the pictures on these pages show, produced some splendid news photography. It was, in fact, finer than most people suspected at the time, for before it could be published it had to be clumsily reproduced by engravings or crude lithographs, and few people ever saw the original photograph.

Despite its successes, the daguerreotype was soon dead. It foundered on a popular craze: the people who had been satisfied with a simple silver portrait of themselves in 1845 wanted in 1855 a hundred portraits on visiting cards to give their friends. This could be done only by making negatives from which many positive pictures could be taken. So the collodion wet-plate negative, paper positive method (which was to photograph the Civil War) took over. But the daguerreotype lit a fire of enthusiasm for photography that has not died yet.

FIRE RUINS of the American Hotel in Buffalo, destroyed in 1850, are surveyed by the curious. The ghostly images are those of people who moved during the lengthy exposure.

4. THE LURE
OF NEW LANDS

Moses and Stephen Austin had the dream. Father and son, they saw a new little world of their own in Texas, where men could live at peace with their neighbors and with no barriers to their progress. This was the dream of many an American. Texas was the Western Star, hanging over the horizons of land-hungry Americans, many of whom would always contend that the vast area had been part of the original Louisiana Purchase. Spain had thought otherwise, and listed Texas among the provinces lost in the Mexican uprising of 1821.

But there was room enough for all in this big country, in the vast, unending loneliness of a region in which an opening in the woods could be a plain extending for miles. All the yarns that were spun about "Old Kaintuck" were told again now about Texas. "Everything is bigger here than in the United States," a newcomer said.

It was Moses Austin who paved the way for American settlement, but he did not live to see it happen. In his lifetime he had been a Philadelphia dry-goods merchant, a mine operator in Virginia, a judge in the Louisiana Territory, a banker in Missouri. Always on the move, always seeking a better way of life, he kept one jump ahead of the advancing frontier. After his St. Louis bank failed in the early 1800s, the most promising land Moses Austin found was across the border of Spanish Mexico, some 500 miles away. Early in 1821 he received permission from the Spanish commandant-general to settle 300

FIRST INHERITOR of the presidency, John Tyler, who succeeded the dead Harrison in 1841, displays mementos of his one term—including a map of newly annexed Texas.

families in Texas. But on his return trip to Missouri he was caught by wretched weather in a corner of his promised land, and he took sick. Although he managed to get back home, he died in June.

His son carried through the colonization plan. Stephen Austin was only 29 years old, but he was a steady, thoughtful man who had been a director of the bank owned by his family and a member of the Missouri territorial legislature. He was reluctant to pull up stakes and travel to Texas, but his father had asked on his deathbed that Stephen carry on. In 1822 Stephen Austin led a group of settlers to Texas.

This was no hit-or-miss migration. Whole families were enrolled in Austin's "Old Three Hundred." They intended to become citizens of Mexico, which had just won its independence. In token of their good faith, they even adopted Catholicism, as Mexican law required. They bought land at 12.5 cents an acre and settled down to establish a model colony—law-abiding, literate and, within a few years, prosperous.

By 1832, some 20,000 Americans had flooded over the border—and some of these, in violation of Mexican law, had brought slaves with them. These were a different breed from the Old Three Hundred, with their own ways and wishes—and, quite often, a marked hostility toward Mexicans. But this flood of newcomers had settled the fate of Texas, and even the Mexicans knew it. They saw that the Americans had schools and the Mexicans none, that the Americans were getting land and building houses while the few Mexicans in Texas stayed poor. Mexico was letting a treasure go by default. It had turned down Secretary of State Henry Clay's offer of purchase in the 1820s, and another offer from Andrew Jackson in 1829. Now, Mexico's increasingly corrupt regime suddenly tightened its control over Texas. It prohibited further immigration by Americans, sent troops into the region and tried to administer the whole vast province from Mexico City. The inevitable happened. The Americans—Texians, they were beginning to call themselves—rose in revolt (see pages 92-93), and in March 1836, at the little hamlet of Washington, they declared themselves a free republic.

Already blood had flowed. At the sun-baked old mission of the Alamo, almost 200 Americans had been wiped out in a desperate hand-to-hand battle with a vastly superior force of Mexicans. The blood-soaked fortress had become a page in the history of the Republic of Texas—and a rallying cry to Americans who rushed to help the young republic. Another clash occurred at Goliad, where some 350 more Texians died. The climactic battle came at San Jacinto on April 21, 1836. It was led by Sam Houston on the flats before the town that now bears his name, and in 18 minutes it changed the whole character of the war. Charging to the cry "Remember the Alamo," Houston's troops administered a smashing defeat to the surprised Mexicans. When the fighting was over, the Mexican commander was a fugitive (he was caught the next day and later freed), and the struggle for independence was won.

H OUSTON'S had been a spectacular career. In his teens he had donned loincloth and blanket to live for a time as an Indian. During the War of 1812 he had fought under Andrew Jackson and had been badly wounded. At 24 he was a government agent to the Cherokee chiefs under Monroe; at 30 he was elected to the House; at 34 he was named governor of Tennessee. At 35 he was an heir apparent to President Andrew Jackson, and seemingly at the

Frontiersman James Bowie, surrounded by pistols, is depicted fighting to the death in defense of the Alamo. Actually, it is not known exactly how he died—only that he had been sick before the Texas fort fell. According to one legend, he fired his pistols until the Mexicans ran him through; then they hoisted his body on bayonets and paraded in celebration.

peak of his career. Around the polling booths of Tennessee he reared tall in the saddle of his dapple-gray horse, a high black beaver hat on his head.

His fall was dramatic. It appears that this flamboyant, extravagantly picturesque and romantic figure was beloved of all women except his wife. She was a Tennessee society beauty, 17 years younger than he; they were wed in 1829, during his gubernatorial administration, and then separated, without explanation, within a few months. Despite Houston's insistence that his marriage was a private affair, the public reaction when he left her forced his resignation as governor. He wrote afterward that he was in "an agony of despair" and tempted to end his "worthless life" when suddenly an eagle swooped down near his head, soared aloft and was "lost in the rays of the setting sun." Houston took this as a portent. "I knew," he wrote, "that a great destiny waited for me in the West."

By any standard, Houston's was a great destiny. As the first president of the Republic of Texas he proved to be as skillful an executive as he had been a military commander. He pounded a government out of the rawest of raw materials and built Texas into a nation. Although the new country was without cash or credit, dogged by vengeful Mexicans, hounded by marauding Indians and suspect in the eyes of the great nation to the north, which remembered the dreams and plottings of Aaron Burr, Houston nevertheless persevered. In the end he saw Texas recognized as a power by other powers, kept the peace and held the vast treasure intact for the United States.

A terrific explosion on the U.S.S. Princeton in 1844 kills two Cabinet officers and several others. The tragedy produced unforeseen results. The following year the Secretary of the Navy, convinced—in part by the Princeton disaster—that the navy needed reorganization, took over an old army post, and on October 10, 1845, opened the Naval Academy at Annapolis.

T HE admission of Texas into the American Union was the crowning achievement of Houston's career. Certainly it was the most difficult. To attain his end, Houston used a combination of persuasion, cajolery, international politicking and well-timed threats—to say nothing of grudging cooperation with his old enemy John C. Calhoun. All these tactics were necessary, for by the 1830s the ramifications of "the Texas question" extended far beyond Texas. It was slavery, rather than Texas, that was at issue.

Southerners saw in this vast land an opportunity to turn the Union's balance of power in their favor. Northerners, therefore, soon saw annexation as a mere extension of the slave power. Even John Quincy Adams, who as President had tried to buy Texas, now looked upon annexation as nothing but a Southern plot. To the bait held out by Sam Houston—the vast and growing market of Texas for Yankee manufactured goods—most of the North displayed a marked indifference.

The Republic of Texas first sought admission to the American Union in 1836. Andrew Jackson, aware of the growing acrimony over the slave question, was publicly unmoved by Houston's entreaties. The best he could offer the young republic was recognition. The same step also was taken, ominously, by England; for the British, Texas offered a glorious opportunity to secure a new market and to bar the southward growth of the United States.

Thereafter Sam Houston, first citizen of Texas whether in or out of office, applied the strategic principle with which he had won San Jacinto: "Concentrate, retreat and conquer." If scorned by the United States, he said, Texas must seek the protection of "some other friend." So he held out tempting inducements in well-publicized negotiations with the British. Although Houston wrote privately to a friend in England that "When we get our hand in the Lion's mouth, my rule is to get it out . . . easily," his public statements were designed for American consumption. Texas was awaiting annexation "as a bride adorned for her espousal," Houston had written. But if the United States was indifferent, Texas would look elsewhere for acceptance and build up a rival power along the Pacific. Only annexation, Houston intimated, could halt this possibility.

John Tyler, a President of more courage and enterprise than history has credited him with, moved into action. Tyler was a Virginian, a Democrat who believed firmly in the Jeffersonian doctrines of states rights and strict construction of the Constitution. But he was also a man of the utmost independence, a maverick for much of his life. Time after time he found himself at odds with his colleagues—but almost always because national political alignments were shifting, and rarely because he varied from his fundamental philosophy. He had supported Jackson for President—but as a senator he voted to censure Jackson over the President's removal of the deposits of the Bank of the United States. When Virginia Democrats insisted that he vote to expunge the censure, Tyler promptly resigned from the Senate. In 1840 this former Democrat accepted the Whig nomination as Vice President and was elected. One month after the inauguration, Tyler inherited Harrison's presidency and Whig Cabinet. Within six months all the Cabinet members but Secretary of State Daniel Webster resigned, leaving Tyler, in effect, a President without a party.

Nevertheless, his Administration was notable for its accomplishments, ranging from the reorganization of the navy to the ending of the Seminole War and the opening of China to foreign trade. For besides being a man of integrity, Tyler was a man of charm, a quality that helped him get things done even in a politically hostile world. "In his official intercourse with all men, high or low, he was all that could be asked: approachable, courteous, always willing to do a kindly action, or to speak a kindly word," said a man who knew him.

Few acts of the Tyler Administration were more important than the annexation of Texas. It was accomplished by a combination of accident and acumen. Tyler, although he favored annexation, had at first to placate the Northern Whigs who had agreed to serve in his Cabinet. Therefore, he had to move with great care to avoid the accusation that he was playing the Southern game with regard to Texas. Then, on February 28, 1844, fortune took a hand. A distinguished list of notables, including the President, boarded the U.S.S. *Princeton,* a revolutionary propeller-driven steam frigate, for a ceremonial trip down

Sentries guard a blacksmith shop in Washington-on-the-Brazos as a convention of Texans assembles within. With curtains draped over the windows to keep out the cold, they agreed that they had "reached that point at which forbearance ceases to be a virtue," and proceeded to declare their independence.

the Potomac River. During the voyage, the vessel's 12-inch cannon were demonstrated. One of them exploded, killing, among others, Secretary of State Abel P. Upshur, Secretary of the Navy Thomas W. Gilmer and a New York state senator named David Gardiner. There was a surprising aftermath to this tragedy. Tyler, a widower, had been wooing Senator Gardiner's daughter Julia. The accident almost literally threw them together; the pace of the courtship speeded up, and four months later the 54-year-old President married the beautiful 24-year-old girl.

Politically, the explosion had more far-reaching results. With two positions in his official family suddenly made vacant, Tyler seized the opportunity to reorganize the entire Cabinet. He named not a single Northerner or Whig—and John C. Calhoun came out of retirement and took the post of Secretary of State. Calhoun—and Tyler—had just one thought in mind: to insure the admission of Texas into the Union.

In his eagerness, Calhoun overplayed his hand. He infuriated the North by declaring that the annexation of Texas was essential both to the safety of the South in the Union and to the survival of slavery. When his proposed treaty of annexation was presented, the Senate voted it down.

But the forces building up behind annexation were becoming almost overpowering. A short time before the Senate vote, the retired Andrew Jackson had taken a hand in the matter. He had summoned to the Hermitage the one man who could dramatize the Texas question most effectively, James Knox Polk, ardent advocate of annexation. With Old Hickory's backing, Polk was named the Democratic candidate for the presidency. In the fall election he defeated Henry Clay, the Whig candidate, who had hedged on the Texas issue.

But Tyler was still President—and he was now convinced that the country wanted to annex Texas. He was determined to accomplish that end. If he and Calhoun could not do it in the regular way, they would do it by irregular means: they would bring Texas into the Union by joint resolution. A treaty would require the approval of two thirds of the Senate. A resolution could be adopted by a simple majority of both houses. That was an easier matter; when the resolution came to a vote it passed in both House and Senate.

Yet all was not certain. Though Texas was admitted—with slavery guaranteed, and with the privilege of splitting itself up into five states if it desired—there was still a question. "What will Houston do?" asked the dying Jackson.

The currency of the new Republic of Texas was handsomely engraved but not worth much. Within a few years of independence the nation's issue of interest-bearing promissory notes was valued at only 50 cents on the dollar—and the non-interest-bearing "red backs" (left) had plunged to eight and 10 cents.

A cartoon satirizes Rhode Island's Dorr Rebellion of the 1840s, portraying its leader, Thomas Dorr, as a fat Napoleon. The uprising was aimed at a constitution that limited the vote to men owning $134 worth of land. It ended in an abortive show of arms. But it led to a new state constitution which liberalized the franchise. Dorr was jailed for treason, but later freed.

Had the negotiations with England gone too far? A letter went out from the Hermitage to Houston; on June 6, 1845, an answer was returned. Texas would join the States. "All is safe at last," Jackson said.

On February 16, 1846, the Lone Star flag of the Republic of Texas was lowered slowly to the ground and the Stars and Stripes mounted the pole. Sam Houston now could exult that his only object all along had been to flirt with the United States until its desire for Texas grew irresistible. "If ladies are justified in making use of coquetry" to get husbands, he said, well pleased with himself, could he not be excused for "making use of the same means" for bringing Texas into the Union?

Annexation of Texas did not settle all the boundary problems that confronted the young nation in the 1840s. The northern borders had been a source of controversy at both ends of the continent. As far back as 1837, the smoldering Canadian frontier had leaped into flames. That year a rebellion broke out in Canada over popular demands for greater self-government. It aroused instant sympathy among Americans, who saw it as a belated echo of their own fight for freedom from the mother country, and who hoped that once they were independent of Britain the Canadians would unite with the United States. Northern Vermont and New York were the focal points of American aid to the Canadian rebels, and international violence soon flared near Niagara Falls. Canadian militia crossed the Niagara River by dark on December 29, 1837, and set fire to the *Caroline*, a small American steamer that had been ferrying supplies to the rebels. In May of the next year, Yankees retaliated by burning a Canadian vessel on the St. Lawrence River. Only British restraint and stern enforcement of American neutrality laws by President Van Buren prevented the pyramiding of such incidents into open Anglo-American warfare.

But the squabbling took a more serious turn in the wilderness along the Maine-Canada border. There, in 1838, burly lumberjacks from the United States and the Canadian province of New Brunswick broke each other's heads over who was entitled to cut the timber in the disputed territory. In 1839 a Maine land agent named Rufus McIntire, trying to eject Canadian lumbermen from disputed territory under authority granted him by the state, was arrested by the Canadians. Militia was called up on both sides, and the U.S. Congress appropriated $10 million and voted to raise a force of 50,000 men to meet the emergency. This dispute was called the "Aroostook War," but fortunately no blood was shed. General Winfield Scott, sent by Van Buren to the danger area, was able to arrange a truce, to last until the entire question could be settled by a boundary commission.

SHORTLY after Tyler took office in 1841, his first Secretary of State, Daniel Webster, reopened negotiations with Britain on the long-standing northeastern boundary question. During the wholesale resignation of the Whig Cabinet in September 1841, Webster had stayed on. A special British negotiator, Lord Ashburton, arrived in Washington in the spring of 1842 and serious talks got under way. Webster, and the business community of which he was always mindful, wanted peace. So, in a series of long, informal conversations, in which Tyler himself took a hand at one critical juncture, Webster settled the Aroostook question by fixing on a compromise boundary between Maine and New Brunswick. As the compromise gave a slight edge to Britain, the British in exchange conceded the claim of the United States to certain lands along the northern border of New Hampshire and in the vicinity of Lake Champlain.

In another important provision of the settlement, the British relinquished their claimed right to search American vessels suspected of carrying slaves; the United States, in turn, agreed to establish squadrons that would halt and search ships flying the American flag. With the treaty's determination of the boundary line from Lake Superior to the Lake of the Woods, America's northern border was finally determined as far west as the Rocky Mountains. Neither Webster nor Ashburton showed any great desire to tangle with the thorny question of Oregon, and the Webster-Ashburton treaty confirmed by the Senate in August 1842 made no mention of that outstanding problem.

B UT the Oregon question had to be settled. For years that vast, rich wilderness of 500,000 square miles had been disputed territory, claimed at various times not only by the United States and Britain but also by Spain and Russia. By 1818, however, only the first two nations were seriously contending for the region; that year they agreed to occupy the land jointly. In 1827 this arrangement was renewed for an indefinite period, subject to cancellation on one year's notice.

In 1825 the powerful Hudson's Bay Company had established the trading post of Fort Vancouver on the north bank of the Columbia River. The company cut timber, organized far-ranging troops of fur trappers and cemented relations with the Indian tribes.

American settlers hung back. The difficulty of travel, and the isolation from the rest of the country enforced by the fearsome wall of the Rockies, made the lands east and west of the Mississippi far more attractive to pioneer farmers. By 1839 there were only about 100 Americans in Oregon.

But the stage had already been set for a massive migration, and it was only a question of time before it began. The Great Plains had been explored; the South Pass through the Rockies was open; the pathways were established and ready. Slowly the word reached the East—a rich land, rivers teeming with fish, and endless forests lay waiting for someone to claim them. By 1843, hundreds of Americans were succumbing to the "Oregon fever." They packed their belongings and their families into sturdy wagons, yoked up their oxen and headed out on the long trek to the Pacific.

The laborious and perilous journey started for most travelers at Independence, Missouri, and then followed the winding route of the rivers—the Missouri, the Platte, the Sweetwater—for almost 1,000 miles through the Great Plains to the mountains. The route cut through the Rockies by way of the broad South Pass, then took the route of the Snake River into modern Idaho, over the dangerous and difficult Blue Mountains, and at last reached Fort Vancouver—a distance from Independence of more than 2,000 miles. The journey took an average of six months, and the route was beset by fierce cold in winter and broiling sun in summer. Often the migrants ran low on food. Draft animals died of overexertion; wagons broke down and a grim list of diseases took their toll of the pioneers: dysentery, scurvy, respiratory ailments, cholera. Many a venturesome traveler who had lightheartedly set out from Missouri on a bright spring morning found a final resting place on the frozen bank of a lonely river in the West. "The cowards never started," a folk saying went, "and the weak died on the way."

During the 1830s the trail was taken chiefly by traders, later by a growing

Daniel Webster (right) is lampooned for yielding part of Maine to British Lord Ashburton in 1842. He was also much criticized for his heavy drinking and the huge fees he got for backing special interests in Congress. Said cleric Theodore Parker, "Selfish egotism is the only continuous thread I find running through the crooked life of this famous American."

number of Protestant and Catholic missionaries to the Nez Percé, Flathead and Cayuse Indians. In 1836 there arrived at Fort Vancouver a party of nine, including a young doctor, Marcus Whitman, and a Presbyterian clergyman, Henry Spalding. Both men brought their wives: the lovely blonde Narcissa Whitman and the tall, dark Elizabeth Spalding. These two were the first white women to travel the Oregon Trail, and the details of their difficult trek have been preserved in Narcissa Whitman's journal. Married just before starting out for the West, Narcissa and Marcus Whitman spent their honeymoon on the trail. One by one they had to discard precious possessions to lighten the load on their draft animals. When an axle broke they had to cut their wagon in half, and in the two-wheeled cart that remained they traveled as far as Idaho. They completed the trip to Oregon on horseback. Six months after she arrived at Fort Vancouver, Narcissa was delivered of the first white American child born west of the continental divide.

Fort Vancouver, with its bristling cannon and its palisade of sharp-pointed posts rising 20 feet into the air as protection against attackers, was presided over by one of the most remarkable and powerful figures of the Northwest. He was a medical man named Dr. John McLoughlin, and he ruled like a benevolent baron over a little empire of traders, half-breeds, Indians and immigrant Englishmen. The Indians called this six-foot-four-inch Canadian "the white-headed eagle" because of the masses of snowy hair that flowed around his austerely handsome features.

As the region's chief factor of the great Hudson's Bay trading company, McLoughlin's job was to keep American traders out of Oregon. "They must be opposed as much as we can," he had written in 1826, and all the force of his organization was concentrated on this goal. That he was firmly entrenched, none who saw his empire could doubt—with its efficient personnel, its ample stores, its farm of 3,000 acres, the 40-odd buildings within the stockade, offices, warehouses, assembly halls, workshops for mechanics, coop-

Travelers heading westward gather around a fire during the "Great Migration" of 1843. Despite the cheerfulness of this scene the route was difficult—menaced, in Horace Greeley's words, by "snowy precipices" and "gnawings of famine." The editor said: "This migration . . . wears an aspect of insanity."

ers, blacksmiths and wheelwrights. All this was the work of one man. The Indians were his allies. Many of his men married Indian women; his own wife was part Chippewa, and he demanded that the Indian wives be treated with respect. He was a symbol of justice to the red men, as well as the white. Because of him, no tribe had made war against the whites; in the end, partly because of him, there would be no war between America and England.

Despite his opposition to American traders, McLoughlin gave a cordial welcome to the settlers and missionaries who arrived at Fort Vancouver, exhausted after their long trip from the East. He had greeted the Whitmans in friendship, and in the same fashion he greeted those who followed, lending them enough food to last them through their first winter and giving valuable advice about the new country.

The newcomers were glad to have McLoughlin's help, but they were in no mood to accept British sovereignty or nationality. Moreover, good land south of the Columbia—where the early American settlers had staked out their farms—was becoming harder to find, and the new arrivals were unwilling to accept British claims to the land north of the river. It was apparent that a clash was in the making.

In 1843, when there were about 1,500 Americans in Oregon, a small group of them—following the traditional American pattern—decided to create a government. They met on July 5 in an old Hudson's Bay warehouse at Champoeg, in the Willamette Valley, to draw up a provisional constitution for self-protection until the United States should see fit to establish its sovereignty over the area. If Congress would not act, the people would. Back East as well, the people took a hand in the affair. Although the United States had several times offered to settle the boundary at the 49th parallel, representatives of six Mississippi Valley states now demanded the entire Oregon territory all the way to latitude 54° 40'. The nation soon took up the cry "54-40 or Fight!" and in 1844 elected a President committed to that line.

Marcus Whitman is killed by Indians in 1847. Missionary Whitman might have saved himself but for his zeal. Ordered to close his mission in 1842, he set out for the East to appeal. It was a harrowing trip through the dead of winter. But he got the order changed and went back to Oregon—and death.

James Knox Polk of Tennessee was the most notable President between Jackson and Lincoln. An intense, dedicated, rigidly self-disciplined man, he was of the same unyielding Scotch-Irish stock as Jackson and Calhoun. It is no accident that the last words Jackson ever wrote were in a letter of advice and "ardent friendship" to Polk. Despite the Whigs' taunt of "Who is James K. Polk?" and their attempts to dismiss him as a dark horse, the Democrats knew Polk very well. The new President had been a Jacksonian congressman at 29, a man who by one account had missed but a single day of work in 14 years, a bitter opponent of the United States Bank, an able Speaker of the House, a notable storyteller and a governor who had saved Tennessee from bankruptcy. At 49, he was the youngest man yet to assume the presidency.

Polk early found the office to be "no bed of roses," as he noted in his diary. He felt himself continually harassed by people: a diplomat announcing the birth of a prince; would-be officeholders; delegations of Indians; Sunday-school children wanting to sing to him; tourists pumping his hand or staring at him as he ate or peeking into the presidential bedroom. Only after midnight could he take care of the work that required concentration. His health became wrecked by the strain of the presidency.

The measure of Polk's success is that he accomplished so much in one term—which was all that he would consent to serve. He was not an easy man to deal with. Having disclaimed ambition in himself, he was continually smelling it and scotching it in others. Any Cabinet member who wanted to become President was expected to resign, and he tended to diagnose presidential fever in any general who opposed him. In spite of these crotchets, he had a remarkably high degree of success in achieving his goals.

Polk entered office knowing exactly what he wanted: treasury reform, tariff reduction, settlement of the Oregon boundary, and California. In his territorial ambitions, Polk rode the surging wave of American imperialism, an almost mystical roll toward the Pacific which was given dignity by the electric phrase "Manifest Destiny." Coined in 1845, this concept of their nation's inevitable supremacy was enough to satisfy Americans that their role as conquerors of the Western spaces had divine sanction.

IT was Polk's own destiny to be the greatest American empire builder since Jefferson, and he carried through his aims with intense single-mindedness. But he never forgot that he was President of the entire nation. A slaveholder, Polk never sought to extend slavery, but merely the bounds of the Union, north and south, and he battled all agitators on both sides of the slavery issue.

Although he was not averse to a fight, as he was to prove when the time came to deal with Mexico, Polk had no desire to go to war over a difference of 5° latitude in Oregon. With the Mexican war looming, Polk certainly did not intend to take on Great Britain too.

But James Polk was a politician, and mindful of the nationwide sentiment for Oregon that had put him into office. So, in his inaugural message in March of 1845, he reiterated the American claim to the whole of Oregon and proposed giving the required year's notice of termination of the joint-occupancy agreement. Later that year he renewed the standing American offer to compromise the boundary at 49°—in other words, by simply extending the existing Canadian-American border. Richard Pakenham, Britain's minister in Washington, turned him down—whereupon Polk declared that the United

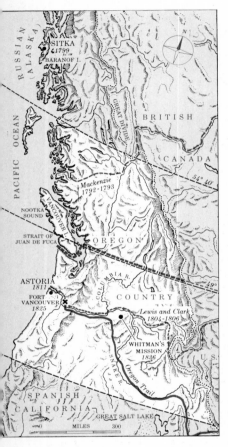

ACCORD BY TREATY ON
THE OREGON BORDER

Oregon, situated between Russian Alaska and Spanish California, was visited by early explorers from the U.S. and Britain—notably the Scot Alexander Mackenzie and the Americans Lewis and Clark. From 1818 on, the two nations ruled the region in white jointly. But by 1842 Americans arriving by the Oregon Trail (bottom) were clamoring for U.S. seizure of the area. The boundary was finally set by compromise at the 49th parallel—an extension west of the existing border—except that Britain got all of Vancouver Island. Important settlements are shown with dates of founding.

States would now accept nothing less than 54° 40'. When a member of Congress expressed anxiety at his defiant tone, Polk responded that "the only way to treat John Bull is to look him straight in the eye."

Not long afterward the British government, growing more and more concerned over the situation, instructed Pakenham to accept 49° as the boundary if Polk would now concur. With a great show of reluctance, the President turned to the Senate for "advice and consent." If the Senate would vote in favor of accepting the latest British offer, Polk said, he would do so. The Senate swiftly gave its approval. The treaty was signed on June 15, 1846.

John McLoughlin, factor for the Hudson's Bay Company in Oregon, shipped more than $100,000 worth of furs to England annually. He sometimes went on buying tours of the region attended by trains of traders and with his part-Indian wife mounted on a horse ajingle with bright silver bells.

I̲N Oregon, John McLoughlin reacted to the changing situation with characteristic grace. As more and more American settlers poured in, he persuaded the Indians not to drive out the invaders. He opened his hospital to the sick, gave his own money to the poor. Much of it he never saw again, for many settlers he had helped moved on to greener fields in California. After the provisional government of Oregon was set up, among those who took the oath was John McLoughlin.

In 1847, Dr. McLoughlin was plunged into grief, for the Whitmans, whom he had befriended, were reported dead at the hands of the Cayuse Indians. For 11 years the work of the missionaries had prospered, as the tribesmen had learned to trust them. But the influx of land-hungry Americans swelled; tension grew and the Indians became alienated. Diseases brought by the immigrants were killing the Indians by the score. When the Whitmans were unable to cure the Cayuse, the tribesmen turned against their old friends. In November 1847, the Indians massacred 14 members of the mission.

After the signing of the treaty that finally settled the boundary conflict with England, the Polk Administration's interest in Oregon subsided for a time. The question of providing a government was intimately tied up with the question of slavery, and it was not until 1848 that a free-soil government was established in the territory.

Dr. McLoughlin, now a full-fledged American citizen, was quick to feel the ingratitude of the people he had befriended. They distrusted him as a despot; they feared him as a Catholic; on a technicality, they robbed him of all the land he personally possessed. He had resigned as factor of the Hudson's Bay Company, and the British had attacked him as a traitor. "For what?" he cried in a document written near the end of his life. "Because I acted as a Christian, saved American citizens, men, women and children from the Indian tomahawk and enabled them to take farms to support their families. . . ."

Old and sick, he addressed a pathetic plea to a rising young Oregon politician. "I might better have been shot 40 years ago than to have lived here and tried to build up a family and an estate in this government," he said. "I became a citizen of the United States in good faith. I planted all I had here, and the government confiscated my property. Now what I want to ask of you is that you will give your influence after I am dead to have this property go to my children. I have earned it as other settlers have earned theirs, and it ought to be mine and my heirs."

The young leader later fought in the Oregon legislature to fulfill this trust. Eventually the McLoughlin lands were restored to their rightful owners. But it was too late to help John McLoughlin. The "Father of Oregon" died in 1857, disillusioned and almost penniless.

A British cartoon jeers at American claims to the entire West. Cries John Bull to Brother Jonathan: "What! you young yankee-Noodle, strike your own father?" And some Americans considered Oregon a bag of "hills, hollers, rocks, rivers, vallies . . . wild onions and wild Indians" not worth fighting for.

Texans caught in a border raid draw beans in a deadly game. Mexicans shot 17 who drew black beans.

The Lone Star's turbulent birth

IF ever there was a land that seemed destined for conflict it was the Texas of the early 19th Century. Though part of the Spanish colony of Mexico, it was hundreds of miles from the government in Mexico City; after a century of desultory colonization it was still sparsely settled. But across its vague northern boundary were many Americans to whom this rich, empty land was an irresistible temptation. In the early 1800s, while Mexico was breaking away from Spain, scores of restless Yankees left for the new country. Throughout the Southwest "Gone to Texas"—soon shortened to "GTT"—became the familiar explanation for a missing face. By the 1830s Americans outnumbered the Mexican settlers and were talking about independence.

Belatedly the Mexican government took harsh measures to restore control. Immigration was banned and troops dispatched to collect heavy taxes. In 1835 the Americans rebelled.

The Texas revolution was characterized by ineptness on both sides. It lasted six months, but there were only three major encounters. The numerically superior Mexicans won two but lost the third—and the war—to a small force led by a former Tennessee governor named Sam Houston *(opposite)*.

But even after Texas had its independence, there was no peace. Border incidents—like the raid on Mier, Mexico, which culminated in the bizarre lottery above—plagued the region for years. Even after Texas was annexed to the United States in 1845 the violence continued. The U.S. and Mexico would have to fight a war before tranquility would finally return to turbulent Texas.

THE HERO OF SAN JACINTO, Sam Houston leads his arm in the charge that won Texas its independence. This pic ture by S. Seymour Thomas is in the San Jacinto Museum

The fateful Yankee invasion of a colorful land

THE Texas to which the first American settlers came was a vast, largely vacant region with only a few scattered oases of Mexican civilization. The brightest of these was San Antonio, in southern Texas, which had grown from a cluster of missions to become capital of the territory and home of the Spanish governor's sophisticated court. To festive dances in the ballroom of the Governor's Palace came the town's elite, sparkling and bejeweled in high Spanish fashion. Mexican settlers and Indians converted by the Franciscan monks also lived there, farming and raising sheep in sunny serenity. Their Spanish customs remained heavily imprinted on the town long after Texas broke away from Mexico. In 1844, when the wandering artist Theodore Gentilz saw the scenes below and opposite, life in San Antonio had not changed perceptibly in half a century.

Among the earliest Americans to settle down in this land was a group of nearly 300 led by a 29-year-old Missourian named Stephen Austin. Austin was anything but a rebel. He required his followers to become Mexican citizens and to convert to Roman Catholicism, and he tried earnestly to get along with his Mexican neighbors. But other, rowdier Americans followed, and their ambitious search for prosperity inevitably carried the seeds of conflict. Within 15 years Texas was torn by war.

STEPHEN F. AUSTIN, usually a peaceable man, prepares for trouble upon hearing of an Indian attack from a wounded scout (*above*). The lines on the floor are land survey results.

FANDANGO DANCERS have a lively evening at the Governor's Palace in San Antonio. The palace, which has been restored, was the center of a gay social life in the days of Spanish rule.

TORTILLA MAKERS squat *(above)* on the floor of a cool thick-walled kitchen in San Antonio. In this area, houses were built with heavy walls and narrow windows to keep out the heat.

SKILLFUL RIDERS tangle in San Antonio's Military Plaza in the annual *corrida de la sandia*, or. watermelon race. In this event, contestants tried to wrest the melon from one another.

The fierce flames of revolt

The revolt which flared in October of 1835 consisted of a few skirmishes climaxed by an episode of high drama. In the battle of the Alamo a handful of heroic men including Davy Crockett, seen above wielding his rifle "Old Betsy," forged a legend of bravery as bright—if foolhardy—as any in American history.

The battle probably should not have been fought at all. In December, Texans stormed and took San Antonio, then gradually drifted away. In February, Mexican dictator Santa Anna marched against the town, whose garrison of Texans then numbered fewer than 200. Instead of retreating, the defenders stubbornly retired to the old mission of the Alamo. For 12 days they stood off 3,000 Mexicans, but the result was foredoomed. By the end every defender had been cut down. Texas had suffered a bloody loss. But the courage shown at the Alamo provided the inspiration that led the rebels to final victory.

The smashing triumph
of a cautious commander

THE Lone Star Republic's birth occurred at the Texans' darkest moment. Even as the Alamo was being besieged, 46 delegates of the American settlers were drawing up the legal framework for the new nation. First they wrote a Declaration of Independence, then a Constitution. They made Sam Houston commander of their disorganized forces and, undeterred by Santa Anna's success, told Houston to go out and defeat the Mexicans.

Before the delegates could even get home to trade pen for sword, the invaders struck again. Eighty-five miles from the smoking Alamo, Mexican troops fell on two forces of Texans near the town of Goliad. About 350 Texans were captured—and almost all were murdered.

Texans yearned for revenge, but first Houston had to build an army. Feinting, dodging, falling back, he skillfully avoided the advancing Mexicans until he could whip his own unruly recruits into fighting shape. For 40 days he retreated. Then on April 21 he was ready. With 800 whooping Texans Houston burst into the Mexican camp on the plain of San Jacinto. The Texans, outnumbered almost two to one, routed the disorganized Mexicans in 18 minutes of furious hand-to-hand battle, and then captured their bedraggled commander. It was a brilliant exploit—and when it was all over, Houston had become a hero and Texas an independent nation.

ARROGANT DICTATOR Antonio López de Santa Anna is pictured after he overthrew the Mexican government in 1833 and became president. He called himself the "Napoleon of the West."

HUMBLED PRISONER at San Jacinto, Santa Anna stands before Sam Houston, who suffered an ankle wound during the fight. The Mexican general fled the battlefield in a private's uniform but was captured and then identified when Mexican prisoners saluted him. Houston spared Santa Anna's life despite the arguments of those with the rope (*left*) who wanted to lynch him.

5. IN THE HALLS OF THE MONTEZUMAS

THE news came slowly at first. The nation knew that President James Knox Polk thought war with Mexico was possible and that General Zachary Taylor and his men had been sent into disputed territory near the Rio Grande. But the news that war had actually broken out was a shock, bursting like a bombshell over Congress and the country in that spring of 1846.

Morally the Mexican War has been viewed as the least justified, though materially it turned out to be the most successful, of any conflict in American history. Many Americans saw it as nothing but a barefaced plot to extend slavery. Many saw nothing glorious about invading a virtually helpless neighbor state and seizing over 500,000 square miles of its territory. Yet this chapter in American history might have been a good deal darker if the more rabid exponents of Manifest Destiny—who were demanding all of Mexico by the war's end—had been given their way. Polk was hardly prepared to go that far, but he did want leverage to buy the Mexican territories of New Mexico and California.

American-Mexican relations had been bad for almost two decades. Polk had some reason to say in his war message, "The cup of forbearance had been exhausted." In 1835, a year before the Alamo, the Mexicans had brutally executed 22 Americans. Others were tossed into prisons; treaties were ignored; debts were left unpaid; American ships were captured and detained, and American citizens were robbed and murdered on the high seas. In 1837 when

AT THE CLIMAX OF TRIUMPH, Mexican War hero General Winfield Scott, on the bay horse at right, rides before the great cathedral into the central plaza of Mexico City.

a Senate resolution called for one last demand upon Mexico for redress of grievances, the President was able to cite no less than 57 of these complaints. The grievances were eventually arbitrated, but relations between the two countries grew steadily worse, particularly after the United States recognized Texas that same year. By 1842 the strain was so great that one American naval officer, convinced there was going to be war, landed and briefly occupied a town in Mexican California before finding out that hostilities had not yet begun.

The United States may well have made its greatest mistake in these years in recognizing the free nation of Mexico as a government at all. The Mexico of those days has justly been called "a late stage in the breakdown of the Spanish Empire." It was continually shaken by revolutions which always ended in plunder. Mexican historians classify the entire period from 1822 to 1848 as one of sheer anarchy. The continual American attempts to enforce treaties and to carry on negotiations were a little like trying to build retaining walls on sand.

When the war finally came, Texas was the cause. Mexico resented the annexation and was convinced that the United States had planned to seize Texas all along. Furthermore Texans and Mexicans disagreed sharply over the location of their disputed mutual border. Mexico had no intention of engaging in full-scale hostilities with the United States over Texas; it was trying to save face and to salvage the remnants of its ailing empire. However, Mexico had previously warned the United States that annexation would amount "to a declaration of war," and when the joint resolution annexing Texas passed Congress in early 1845 there seemed nothing for Mexico to do but to break off diplomatic relations.

STILL, when Polk took the risk of war he had good reason to hope that he could win without fighting. His own conception of Manifest Destiny did not envision the conquest of Mexico proper, but rather of Mexican territory—specifically the great area lying between Texas and the southern limits of the Oregon country.

On May 30, 1846, Polk told his Cabinet that his ultimate purpose was to get California and New Mexico; in fact, for six months he had a man in Mexico negotiating to buy the territories. The President was prepared to go high—as high as $40 million, if need be, and he was sure a sum such as this would ease Mexican pain over its losses.

But just in case it did not, the President was taking no chances. He needed a show of force, so he had earlier dispatched ships to stand off the Mexican coast and had sent an army under General Taylor on a march to the east bank of the Rio Grande, under orders to avoid unfriendly acts but to take "appropriate action" if hostilities should break out. This last step was the culmination of a plan Polk had devised in August 1845. It provided that if Mexico should commence hostilities or cross the Rio Grande in force, Taylor was to attack and drive the invaders back.

Mexico had little choice. In Mexican eyes, Taylor's troops were invaders, wrongfully established on Mexican soil. If Mexico recognized a Texas boundary at all, it saw it as the Nueces River to the east, and not the Rio Grande. Indeed, Mexican troops were already in position on the west bank of the Rio Grande, across from Taylor.

VOLUNTEERS!

Men of the Granite State!

Men of Old Rockingham!! the strawberry-bed of patriotism, renowned for bravery and devotion to Country, rally at this call. Santa Anna, reeking with the generous confidence and magnanimity of your countrymen, is in arms, eager to plunge his traitor-dagger in their bosoms. To arms, then, and rush to the standard of the fearless and gallant CUSHING---put to the blush the dastardly meanness and rank toryism of Massachusetts. Let the half civilized Mexicans hear the crack of the unerring New Hampshire rifleman, and illustrate on the plains of San Luis Potosi, the fierce, determined, and undaunted bravery that has always characterized her sons.

Col. THEODORE F. ROWE, at No. 31 Daniel-street, is authorized and will enlist men this week for the Massachusetts Regiment of Volunteers. The compensation is $10 per month---$30 in advance. Congress will grant a handsome bounty in money and ONE HUNDRED AND SIXTY ACRES OF LAND.

Portsmouth, Feb. 2, 1847.

This poster appeals to volunteers from New Hampshire to enlist in a "Massachusetts" outfit. Massachusetts, largely against the war, was slow in meeting its troop quotas. And despite the poster's glowing reference to the Massachusetts soldier Caleb Cushing, the voters of his state took a dimmer view. When the gallant Caleb ran for governor in 1847, he was defeated.

In the absence of communication lines, Taylor had to act on his own authority. Given a Mexican ultimatum to withdraw or assume responsibility for the consequences, Taylor proceeded to blockade the river. This cut off the Mexican troops' supplies. On April 24, 1846, a force of 1,600 Mexicans crossed the river, encircled 63 Americans and killed, wounded or captured all of them. "Hostilities may now be considered as commenced," Taylor wrote.

On May 11, Polk's "war message" was read to Congress: American blood had been shed "upon the American soil," and a state of war existed "notwithstanding all our efforts to avoid it. . . ."

THE MEXICAN EAGLE BEFORE THE WAR!

This cartoon from the New York weekly "Yankee Doodle" was pro-war. It shows the Mexican eagle before plucking (above) and after (below). In most of the states the initial response to recruiting appeals was so great that Tennessee reported it became "difficult even to purchase a place in the ranks."

CONGRESS was appalled. Among most Americans the war itself was welcome enough. Except in abolitionist circles, which saw the war as a mere plot to extend slavery, war fever was burning high throughout the nation. New York was covered with placards: "Mexico or Death!" and "Ho, for the halls of the Montezumas!" The South was ablaze with excitement, echoing to the march of volunteer companies.

It was the excuse given for the war that disturbed Congress—or at least a part of Congress. William Hickling Prescott's classic story of the brutal Spanish *Conquest of Mexico* had been published not long before and was a bestseller; now here was the United States, on what many regarded as a flimsy pretext, preparing to retrace the bloody tracks of Cortés.

Although the House cast only 14 votes against a declaration of war, the story was different in the Senate. Calhoun, urging that Congress move with "forbearance, dignity and calmness," even argued that there was no war, for according to the Constitution only Congress could declare war. Senator Sam Houston did not want the war; if its purpose was to obtain California, he was sure that could be accomplished through purchase. Thomas Hart Benton, chairman of the Senate Military Affairs Committee, actually agreed with Mexico that the Texas boundary was on the Nueces River, not the Rio Grande. The aging Henry Clay proclaimed the war "unnatural . . . lamentable." Daniel Webster felt it was "founded on pretexts" and "unconstitutional in its origin"; indeed, Polk might well be subject to impeachment for involving the country in it without the consent of Congress. Both Webster and Clay were to lose sons in Mexico.

For men of intellectual self-respect what was hardest to take was the preamble to Polk's message, blaming the hostilities on Mexico. There were many in Washington who knew that Polk was actually considering drawing up a war message even before the news of the hostilities arrived. Calhoun spent the night before the reading of the message feverishly pleading with senator after senator not to vote for war. The next day, white-faced, his eyes blazing, Calhoun told the Senate that before voting for that preamble he would plunge a dagger through his heart.

Other senators could not understand his emotion. But once again, Calhoun was seeing into a darkness that many around him were unable to penetrate. He was aware that thousands of volunteers all over the South hoped to conquer and annex Mexico, and were dreaming of a Southern confederacy which would mean the end of the Union he had loved and served so long. Even if it did not come to this, Calhoun knew that the conquest of Mexico would mean new areas for the United States which the North would never see slave and the South would never see free.

THE MEXICAN EAGLE AFTER THE WAR!

But the antiwar group was in the minority and could not prevail. The Senate, too, voted for war. Once war was declared, the dissidents joined in voting the necessary supplies and in giving their country's cause "a quiet but decided support," as Calhoun said.

Now that he had his war, Polk had to find a general. He had a good one in Taylor but Polk did not trust Taylor, and besides, that general was occupied on the border. What was needed was an over-all field commander—and the fat, flamboyant Winfield Scott, then General-in-Chief of the Army, was the natural choice. Polk ordered Scott into action—immediately. Unfortunately Scott had a habit of writing blunt-spoken letters, and he now wrote one, heavily underlined, to the Secretary of War. He pointed out that he was already working 14 hours a day at the War Department; under the circumstances, he said, he could not possibly outfit an army and go to Mexico before September. "I do not desire to place myself in the most perilous of all positions," he proclaimed, "—*a fire upon my rear from Washington, and the fire in front from the Mexicans.*" That finished Scott. Taylor remained in command of the army in Mexico.

In fact Polk was politically prejudiced from the start against both men. Neither was a Democrat, although Taylor sometimes referred to himself as one. The President, ardent Jacksonian that he was, was convinced, like many dedicated partisans, that the welfare of the country depended on the supremacy of his own party—and as a Jacksonian he was particularly aware of the

MAJOR MOVEMENTS OF
THE WAR IN MEXICO

In the opening campaign, Zachary Taylor cut over the disputed territory from Corpus Christi, took Palo Alto, Matamoros and Monterrey, but came close to defeat at Buena Vista. Meanwhile, Stephen Kearny, heading west from Fort Leavenworth, captured Santa Fe and sent Alexander W. Doniphan south to take Chihuahua. Kearny had a setback at San Pasqual but went on to help Stockton, who had come by sea, and Frémont, who arrived from Oregon, take California. Then Winfield Scott, smashing from Veracruz to Mexico City, achieved the war's final victory.

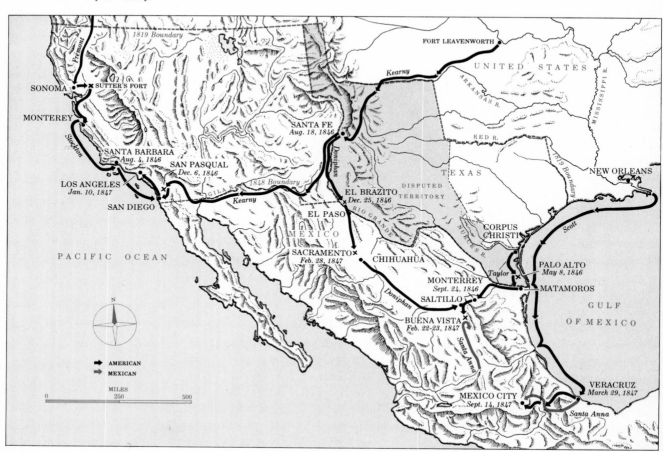

later followed by the Atchison, Topeka and Santa Fe Railroad had a kind of epic quality. They tramped across blazing carpets of flowers, past massive buffalo herds, now and then catching a glimpse of white-frosted mountains. But they also encountered hordes of mosquitoes and buffalo gnats and searing winds, knew parching thirst and weariness, and even found an occasional rattlesnake in their blankets.

Kearny easily occupied Las Vegas, in present-day New Mexico, and issued a proclamation of his intentions, stating that the Americans had come to take possession as friends, not as conquerors. Kearny also promised something which he said the Mexicans had never delivered, protection from the Indians. Furthermore, in this almost wholly Catholic region he promised freedom of religion. By Kearny's own word, a third of his army were Roman Catholics. Priests had even accompanied the American forces, a fact that evoked raging protests in Washington.

On Kearny moved, from town to town, issuing similar statements. At last he quietly took possession of what the men called "Mud Town," the New Mexico capital of Santa Fe, with its adobe buildings. Not a shot was fired in anger, although there was a noisy salute as the Stars and Stripes glided up. The soldiers went to work getting acquainted with the people. Santa Fe was a riot of violent color, the men in slit breeches with silver spurs and flaring capes, the girls barelegged and friendly, the town gay with fandangos.

But Kearny and his dragoons soon pulled out for the march to California, and another force took its place, under Colonel Sterling Price. In December a Mexican plot was uncovered to kill all Americans in the territory. This led to repressive measures by the new commander, then to open rebellion by the New Mexicans, and finally to the assassination of several top American officials. In early February, 1847, Price led an attack against Taos, the focal point of the rebellion. He smashed the rebels completely, and from that time on the area was quiet.

BEFORE Kearny set out he had ordered a small contingent south toward Chihuahua, in Mexico proper, under a popular and respected frontier lawyer, Colonel Alexander Doniphan. By mid-December, after a long, difficult march, Doniphan and his men, now dirty, unshaven and ragged, were moving through the dreary sagebrush country known as Jornada del Muerto, or Dead Man's Journey, in biting cold, without fuel or tents. A Mexican force was waiting for them at El Brazito, about 30 miles from El Paso. The Mexicans sent word that unless the Americans surrendered they would charge. "Charge and be damned!" responded Doniphan.

In the attack that followed the Americans held their fire as they had in past battles, then at close range let loose. Unable to withstand the withering American fusillade, the Mexicans broke and fled. Counting casualties afterward, Doniphan found he had seven men hurt, the Mexicans about 100 killed and wounded. The Americans marched into the large, pleasant settlement of El Paso and rested there through January.

The next month "Doniphan's Thousand," joined by reinforcements, started their 300-mile march to Chihuahua. The country was monotonous and bare. They crossed one desert and then another; occasionally they saw a willow tree. Searing heat alternated with numbing cold. Often there was no water or fuel, but there was no shortage of rattlesnakes and copperheads. On

The woodsman-philosopher Henry David Thoreau expressed his opposition to slavery and the war by refusing to pay his poll tax. Jailed, he emerged calling on all "honest men to rebel and revolutionize." He is sketched above in a "traveling costume" by Daniel Ricketson, an old friend, but a year on Staten Island was as far as he ever got from Walden Pond.

February 27, 1847, they reached a point 15 miles out of Chihuahua. On the Sacramento River, halfway to Chihuahua, the Mexicans were grouped. The Americans attacked on the afternoon of the 28th.

By evening they had cleared the road to Chihuahua, which they occupied peacefully March 2. The story of the fighting was the old one: there had been exactly six casualties for the Americans and reportedly 600 for the Mexicans. In late April, Doniphan, ordered to join Taylor's command, was able to march his men more than 600 miles through enemy territory without encountering one serious challenge.

Kearny, meanwhile, was advancing on California. While he was en route, American irregulars and naval units had taken over most of the region without difficulty, and when this word reached Kearny he sent back all but 150 dragoons. However, by the time he actually reached California in December 1846, some of its Mexican inhabitants had staged an uprising. Los Angeles had been retaken by the Mexicans, and several hundred Spanish-speaking Californians were under arms.

Kearny had to fight his way into San Diego, and at the battle of San Pasqual the small American force was badly mauled. There was further fighting the next month near Los Angeles, but by January 10 the Americans were once again in possession of the town, and all California was secure.

Alexis de Tocqueville, the Frenchman caricatured here, gave Americans a new look at America. He considered New World manners rather free. Servants gossiped with masters, stewards turned down tips, and when a riverboat ran aground the captain slyly told him the sands of the Mississippi were like the French—they "could not stay a year in the same place."

THE war was not yet won; the heart of Mexico proper still remained untouched. Taylor had given no evidence of any over-all plan. But back in Washington a plan was afoot. It was to invade the enemy nation from the sea, at Veracruz on the Gulf Coast, then march straight into Mexico and end the war by taking the capital, Mexico City. The plan had been much discussed in Washington. It was a difficult one, but in the grandiose, eccentric Winfield Scott, Polk had a general who was prepared to carry it out.

From the President's viewpoint there was some risk in entrusting Scott with this task; he was more of a politician than Taylor, although it could readily be seen that the popular appeal of a nickname like "Old Fuss and Feathers" could hardly compare with "Old Rough and Ready." But Polk hoped that a shift of command might bury the presidential aspirations of Taylor stillborn, while coming too late to help Scott. So Polk called upon the man he had once spurned.

The odds seemed impossible, and soldiers everywhere watched with fascination as Scott made his preparations. The American general would be cutting himself off from his base and then would be making a 250-mile march through rough and sometimes fever-ridden country that was defended by a series of almost impregnable strong points. But Scott was confident.

The campaign took six months. There were six victories, five of them bloody. Only the initial landing near Veracruz was uncontested. In this beachhead operation, some 10,000 men, brought down the gulf in transports, crowded into surfboats and were towed close to shore. They then leaped into the water and, holding their guns over their heads, stormed the beach. It was not until hours later that a few Mexican shells were fired. In the days afterward the Americans moved closer, cutting off the Veracruz water supply and occupying the railroad and highways. After a land and sea bombardment failed to take the city, Robert E. Lee constructed a battery 800 yards from the city wall, and from there the Americans put Veracruz under furious siege.

Eighteen days after the landing, the Mexicans raised the white flag of truce.

Leaving an occupying force at Veracruz, the Americans pushed inland. At Cerro Gordo in mid-April, 1847, some 8,500 Americans met a Mexican army under Santa Anna, estimated in size at from 12,000 to 18,000 men. Reconnoitering, Lee found the Mexicans entrenched across the main roadway, with what he called an "unscalable" precipice (actually two hills) on one side and "impassable" ravines on the other.

The first hill was taken after stiff fighting. An initial attack up the steep side of the second failed, but on April 18 the Americans drove the Mexicans off in a furious assault with bayonets, pistols and clubbed muskets. Santa Anna just missed capture, and the Mexicans broke in confusion when a force of Americans suddenly appeared at their rear, having made a long march completely around the enemy position. American casualties were 417, the Mexicans' more than 1,000. Captain Lee received a brevet—an honorary promotion to major—for his exploits. But he wrote: "You have no idea what a horrible sight a field of battle is."

Now Scott marched his army onward toward the Mexican capital. As he got farther and farther from the coast, his position became increasingly dangerous. "Scott is lost," the Duke of Wellington said. But Scott pushed on. Mexico City, surrounded both by marshes and by high, well-fortified ground, was like an island, or a kind of medieval fortress. A wide expanse of jagged lava protected the city to the south, and to the east and north Santa Anna had built mighty fortifications in preparation for the American attack. But under Lee's direction a road was built across the lava bed. Then, while one body of Americans feinted against one of the Mexican strong points, the main force moved across the lava, slipped through a ravine leading to the Mexican rear, and delivered a surprise assault near Contreras. A short, fierce battle resulted. Within 17 minutes the Mexicans had been routed, losing about 700 men and their best cannon. During this fight Brigadier General Franklin Pierce of New Hampshire, who would one day be elected the nation's President, was cruelly hurt in a fall from his horse. He was back in the saddle the next day, his face "white with suffering."

Onward pressed the Americans to the next Mexican defense point, at Churubusco. There sharpshooters and a battalion of American deserters riddled the United States troops for hours, some from hiding places in a field of tall corn, others from the parapets of a convent. In the fighting, Captain Phil Kearny, nephew of the conqueror of New Mexico, lost an arm. The Americans finally turned to the bayonet. Reluctantly the Mexicans fell back. Losses were running higher now: 10,000 in a single day for the Mexicans, 1,000 in two days for the Americans.

WITH his army exhausted and crippled by disease, Scott, seeking a quick end to the fighting, demanded the surrender of Mexico City. Some weeks earlier an American negotiator—Thomas Jefferson's grandson-in-law, the State Department official Nicholas Trist—had arrived in Mexico armed with the American demands for the ending of the war: recognition of the Rio Grande boundary and cession of New Mexico and upper California in return for a $15 million cash payment. Partly in the hope of improving the terms, but mainly because he was in great need of time to organize his defenses, Santa Anna agreed to an armistice.

The armies and settlers were not the only forces moving westward. Hard-working missionaries like this rain-soaked Methodist rider helped open up the region. Sighed one: "I tremble and faint under my burden, having to ride about 6,000 miles annually to preach from 300 to 500 sermons." But everywhere they lifted up the tired hearts of men and they were widely loved.

But the Mexican general had no intention of letting a well-fortified city of 200,000 and an army of 20,000 go by default to 8,000 American invaders. He brought up his best troops and his biggest guns and prepared for a last-ditch battle in the fortified castle of Chapultepec which guarded the city.

There was some inconclusive fighting at Molino del Rey, just outside of Chapultepec, on September 8. Casualties on both sides were heavy: 700 Americans and 2,000 Mexicans. It was said that with a few more of these "victories" there would be little left of the American army.

And the major challenge was still ahead: Chapultepec, the storied Aztec castle on the crags. On this site, Montezuma had lolled beside splashing fountains, and here in the early 16th Century the Spaniard Cortés had come with his pale-faced soldiers. In 1783 a new castle was built by a Spanish viceroy on the ruins of the old. For a while in the early 19th Century the building was abandoned, but around 1840 the Mexicans enlarged and strengthened it, and it became the National Military School, with cadets in gray uniforms and tasseled blue caps drilling in the Tuscan-style structure.

They were still there, and the castle had been heavily fortified. To assail it would be a bloody business. Lee advised against approaching Mexico City by way of Chapultepec; there were other routes. Grant, too, thought the assault would be a frightful mistake. But Grant had not been asked his opinion, and Scott was determined to strike. On September 12 he began bombarding the castle, and early the next morning he moved up his men and charged. There was sharp fighting. Grant led a group that dragged a cannon up close and finally mounted it on a roof. Jackson was later commended for turning back a Mexican attack almost singlehanded. Longstreet led a frontal assault; when he was wounded, the 22-year-old George Pickett seized the flag and urged the men over the ramparts.

Scaling ladders were raised at the castle walls. The fighting was bloody. Even the boy cadets, the youngest of whom was only 13, had thrown themselves into the holocaust, and at the tragic finish they were battling hand-to-hand with the Americans.

The castle fell in just over an hour. Then a tidal wave of Americans flowed into the fort, and the Stars and Stripes rippled out against the morning sky. For the Americans, the price of victory was about 450 men.

BEFORE their eyes now lay the Valley of Mexico. Mountains rimmed it east and west, and below them spread fields yellow with grain. Square in the center stood Mexico City, its buildings gleaming in the morning sunshine.

There was still mopping up to be done around the castle and in the city itself. Still to be reckoned with were breastworks, cannon and a Mexican army which counterattacked furiously when the Americans tried to move into the capital. But after nearly 24 hours and more casualties, Santa Anna was on the run, pulling back toward the north. The American flag soared up in Mexico City's Grand Plaza.

Winfield Scott had done it. His feat was tremendous, a classic of generalship. At no time during Scott's deep penetration of an enemy country, marveled U. S. Grant, did he have a force "equal to one-half of that opposed to him; he was without a base . . . yet he won every battle, he captured the capital, and conquered the government."

Mexico City relaxed into anarchy. In the streets scores of Americans were

Winfield Scott gestures grandly in a patriotic lithograph. He was resplendent and a great gourmet, his tastes sharpened by the best chefs in Europe. Youthful U. S. Grant "thought him the finest specimen of manhood my eyes had ever beheld." Later, a more sophisticated Grant noted that the pompous man was "not averse to speaking of himself, often in the third person."

shot. A Mexican official reported that ragged, dirty United States troops had looted the liquor stores, appearing, he said, "more like brigands than soldiers."

Back home many Americans were still hot for blood. At least one journal proclaimed, "The war must be continued 50 years." One group thought Mexico should be "liberated" from the thralldom of her religion on the ground that no real republic could possibly exist under Catholicism. God, it was said, had decreed Mexico must belong to Protestants and the Union. France had taken Algeria, the Americans had taken Texas, why should they not take Mexico now? One newspaper said most of the Mexican citizens were aboriginal Indians and "must share the destiny of their race—extinction!"

BUT Polk held firm. He had no further designs upon Mexico unless it insisted on protracting the war. Under the Treaty of Guadalupe Hidalgo, which Trist negotiated with the Mexican Government, the war was brought to an end on February 2, 1848.

The Mexican-American border was located along the Rio Grande, New Mexico and California were ceded to the United States, Mexico got $15,000,-000, and the United States assumed some $3,250,000 in Mexican debts to American citizens. Polk was not pleased, for his hand had been forced. Trist actually had no authority to sign for the United States. He had been recalled weeks earlier, on October 6, Polk having succumbed to rumors that Trist had become a political tool of Scott and also that he was planning to weaken on demands for the Rio Grande as the boundary of Texas.

Neither charge was true. In any case Trist was unable to get quick transportation home, so he decided to try for a treaty anyway. He succeeded in getting one that met Polk's original demands, and Polk could only send it to the Senate and denounce Trist helplessly as an "impudent and unqualified scoundrel." The area ceded by the treaty included the present states of California, Nevada and Utah, and parts of Arizona, Wyoming, Colorado and New Mexico. It increased the size of the United States by about 17 per cent—over 500,000 square miles. It was four times the size of Britain, larger than France and Germany combined.

But there was a price. The victory had cost the United States nearly 13,000 lives, only about 2,000 of them lost on the battlefield. It cost the nation perhaps $100 million in military expenditures and made inevitable that greater war which none could win and all would lose.

From his temporary retirement in Lexington, Kentucky, Henry Clay warned the United States against acquiring "foreign territory . . . for the purpose of propagating slavery." The issue had been spelled out clearly a year earlier. In a White House interview in 1846, Polk told Calhoun that slavery would probably never exist in the new provinces he was seeking. At that the South Carolinian replied that he did not wish to extend slavery, but if a treaty with Mexico included a restriction on slavery in the new territories, he would have to vote against it as a matter of principle. Polk kept insisting that the issues of Mexico and slavery should be kept apart. "What connection slavery had with making peace with Mexico," he wrote, "it is difficult to conceive." But Calhoun knew, and from the moment the United States became involved in warfare with Mexico he heard the bell tolling for the death of the Union. "The curtain is dropt," he said, "and the future closed to our view."

AN AVAILABLE CANDIDATE.

A macabre political stab against Zachary Taylor shows him as a candidate for President sitting on top of a mound of soldiers' skulls. But the general's friends sang: "Old Zach's at Monterrey / Bring out your Santa Anner / For every time we raise a gun / Down goes a Mexicanner." Nevertheless Taylor was elected in 1848 mainly because his Democratic enemies were split.

113

"Come all ye gallant volunteers"

THE U.S. that went to war against Mexico in 1846 was a restless nation. "Our people," wrote John C. Calhoun, "are like a young man of 18 . . . disposed for adventure of any description." All over the country, youthful warriors rushed to fill President Polk's call for 50,000 men, and the streets of New York rang with the song, "Come all ye gallant volunteers / Who fear not life to lose." A newspaper predicted that the Mexicans "would be scattered like chaff by the first volley from the Anglo-Saxon rifle. . . ." One colonel, advertising for recruits, described the one-year enlistment as a "pleasant excursion." No one knew of the horrors in store—the terrible heat, the rough terrain, the fierce guerrilla fighters—and few anticipated the rigors of army life, which led some soldiers to rebel and many to desert. To Sam Chamberlain, a footloose 16-year-old from Boston, the war offered a heaven-sent opportunity to play the hero. Sam served first as a volunteer infantryman and then as a regular dragoon. Later he wrote and illustrated his personal war history. His comments and crude but perceptive pictures, seen in these pages, provide a matchless description of the soldier's life in the Mexican War.

MUTINOUS ROOKIES line up for censure. Sam Chamberlain is conspicuous in blonde curls and dark uniform. He complained that "the Company was composed of . . . wild, reckless fellows."

A COLUMN OF DRAGOONS in narrow Devil's Pass (right) is spied on by guerrillas (foreground), who constantly harassed American stragglers, roped and tortured those they captured.

114

Paso él Diablo

STEPPING OUT, hardy troops under General John E. Wool march past Mexicans in San Antonio on September 25, 1846. The force was off to Chihuahua, 450 miles away, and the men lost heart when they learned that "there lay in the way . . . several high ranges of mountains that a goat could not climb, and that [the city] would [require] weeks to flank, through deserts without water." But the plans were changed and it was left to Colonel Alexander W. Doniphan to take the city.

In the gory fighting for Monterrey, Americans storm the Bishop's Palace, a key strong point, and replace the Mexican flag with Old Glory.

A hot battle that "done considerable execution"

DEFEATED MEXICANS leaving Monterrey pass trim U.S. troops, but the Yankees were seldom this neat. After a fight it was said they were so dirty they were hard to tell from the real estate.

ACCORDING to Chamberlain, the "volunteer cavalry . . . possessed fine physiques, and strength combined with activity . . . wild reckless young fellows, with the most inflated ideas of their own personal prowess. . . ." But one observer noted that the poorly trained volunteers "die like sheep." General Winfield Scott listed these troops' faults in a letter to the Secretary of War: "Volunteers . . . eat their *salt* meat raw . . . or, worse than raw, *fried*—death to any Christian man the fifth day; lose or waste their clothing; lie down wet, or on wet ground—fatal to health, and . . . life." Scott also attributed their high losses in combat to "the want of *military* confidence in each other, and . . . of reciprocal confidence between officers and men."

Yet these amateur soldiers performed surprisingly well in the battle of Monterrey, which saw some of the fiercest fighting of the war. The city was very heavily fortified and General Taylor commented grimly that the citadel guarding it "done considerable execution." Possibly prompted by "considerations of humanity," the general agreed to an armistice to let the Mexicans evacuate with their wounded and some supplies, but soon afterward he ordered his refreshed army forward to new battles.

CAVALRYMEN moving away from a threatened attack pause to watch the fire they set burn supplies at Agua Nueva. Chamberlain wrote: "blazing logs were thrown into . . . the houses, bacon and pork thrown on, the large barley stack fired, and soon the whole place blazed up grandly. . . . The hill back of the place fairly glittered with the sheen of Mexican lance points."

WITH SABERS FLASHING, mounted Americans and Mexicans close for combat. In such fighting, some 1,700 Yankees fell on the field of battle, but almost seven times as many soldiers (about 11,300) died of disease and wounds in this war.

A QUIET BIVOUAC on the salt flats gives dragoons a chance to warm themselves around fires. The Mexican weather could be very cold, and many men who had enlisted hoping the climate would be healthful were felled by it instead.

Astride Old Whitey, General Taylor views a battle.

The terrible toll
of a hostile climate

THE soldiers in the Mexican War grew tougher and more skillful as the months passed. They took courage from their officers, most of whom they had selected themselves, and many of whom would gain distinction in the Civil War. Their favorite was Zachary Taylor, "Old Rough and Ready," a carelessly dressed career officer who refused to send his men where he would not go himself. Morale remained remarkably high despite miserable conditions. In one camp so many died of measles, fevers and dysentery that the funeral march "was ever wailing. . . ." But a favorite American slogan remained: "We may be killed, but we can't be whipped."

ACTION AT BUENA VISTA, which took more American lives than any other battle of the war, is shown in Chamberlain's view of the second day's fighting. At the far left, in red shirts and white pants, are the Mississippi Rifles, the heroes of the day. Under the command of Colonel Jefferson Davis, they formed a V into which the lance-carrying Mexican cavalrymen charged. "Steady

boys!" General Taylor shouted. "Steady for the honor of Old Mississippi!" The Mississippians opened fire and did great damage. Then, "profiting by the confusion caused by their ter- rible fire, [they] threw down their rifles. . . . Catching the horses by the bits they backed them onto their haunches and knifed the stupefied riders, who as soon as they could turned and fled."

No-holds-barred warfare behind the lines

THE war's sharpest fighting was not always on the battlefield. In the hostile back country the dreaded guerrillas lay in ambush, many of them convicts freed by the Mexican government in a feverish effort to turn the tide. Working in wolf packs, the irregulars ravaged supply trains and unwary patrols. Lassos and knives were their special weapons, murder and mutilation their trade-marks. United States troops sent to hunt the outlaws learned to give as ruthlessly as they got, and in a dirty and difficult campaign the guerrilla threat was stamped out. But, Sam Chamberlain wrote with distaste, it was a "very disagreeable duty and gained no honor."

SURPRISING A LOOKOUT, Chamberlain's outfit encounters its first guerrilla. "Our road led us into the dry bed of an *arroyo*," wrote Chamberlain. "Right in our path . . . was a guerrilla, clothed entirely in leather and well mounted on a small but wiry mustang." He was overpowered and captured. Later in the campaign he probably would have been killed on the spot.

LIVING BY THE DAGGER, guerrillas murder two U.S. soldiers, using their favorite weapons. The Mexicans would catch their victims with skillful lassos and finish them off with knives.

DYING BY THE SWORD, 17 guerrillas trapped in their hide-out are slain by U.S. troops. Chamberlain, holding a torch at left, wrote, "I acted as a candlestick until the tragedy was finished."

A welcome peace with some grim consequences

BEING WHIPPED for selling liquor to U.S. troops, a sutler, or merchant, sags under the lash. Sam Chamberlain, gagged and bound, sits with others who objected to "the terrible torture."

BOTH sides punished all who had worked with the enemy or otherwise misbehaved. Outrages were frequent, some by the Mexicans, some by Americans—the "lawless volunteers," as one U.S. general called them. Sam Chamberlain complained bitterly of their behavior and of their "impatience of all restraint." His company was once called upon "to protect the wretched inhabitants," as he put it, "and arrest the heroes." Attempts at tightening discipline failed and rising desertions led to stern, merciless punishment. Some deserters (below) were hanged. Orders were issued prohibiting the sale of alcohol, and offenders were punished with 50 lashes. But the damage had already been done. One effect was to discourage completely a move by Mexicans in the northeast to set up a republic under American protection. A Mexican broadside issued at the time commented that they would find the "domination of the Grand Turk . . . kinder." By the war's end, feeling against Americans and those who had fraternized with them ran so high that Mexican killed Mexican at the peace celebrations (right).

AWAITING EXECUTION, U.S. deserters who had joined the Mexicans watch the fighting near Chapultepec, their necks in nooses. They were hanged at the moment of American victory.

SETTLING THE SCORE after the peace, Mexicans murder women (opposite) of Saltillo for befriending American occupiers of the town. Sam Chamberlain drew the grim scene from hearsay.

6. FROM SEA TO SHINING SEA

THE United States had to have California; this was Manifest Destiny. James Polk was determined that no other power should control the fertile province. He felt this way even before his inauguration, before the outbreak of the Mexican War, long before anyone even dreamed of the vast treasures of gold cached away in that sunlit and sleepy land.

Strategically, California was a military necessity. If the United States failed to acquire it from Mexico, someone else might. For in those tentative years before Texas and Oregon became American, California was eyed hopefully by Great Britain, and somewhat less hopefully by France. By the 1840s California was ridden with unrest and ripe for conquest, its scant population ready to throw off the last vestiges of rule from distant Mexico. And there were individual adventurers—as Polk was well aware—with the skill and ambition to exploit the revolutionary spirit for their own ends.

Economically, too, California had to belong to the United States. Shrewd Yankee traders had found the indolent, luxury-loving Californians excellent customers. Once American ships had carried knives, guns, rum and beads to the West Coast. Now they arrived loaded with silk stockings, high-heeled shoes, embroidered scarves and shawls, perfumes and horsehair furniture. To bring this rich trade to an end seemed an intolerable prospect. And certainly if England bought or seized the country, United States commerce would be throttled and America's march to the west halted.

WINNER OF THE WEST, James K. Polk exhibits a thoughtful demeanor in a painting done before the Mexican War, which extended the U.S. to California and the Rio Grande.

On December 2, 1845, Polk invoked the Monroe Doctrine in a message to Congress. He aimed this policy principally at British expansionist moves in Oregon, but Polk was even more worried about the region to the south. Late in October, he had told his friend Senator Benton that America could not sit by and see California fall to a foreign power, and he had written in his diary: "In reasserting Mr. Monroe's doctrine I had California and the fine bay of San Francisco as much in view as Oregon." That same month Polk sent a secret message to Thomas O. Larkin, ostensibly the American consul in California. In reality Larkin was a confidential agent instructed to "exert the greatest vigilance in discovering and defeating any attempt, which may be made by foreign governments to acquire a control over that country."

California was still little known, and such reports as there were varied widely, depending on the travelers' route. Some called it a barren desert, some a mountain country; others spoke of a land of milk and honey. One man wrote: "Here perpetual summer is in the midst of unceasing winter; perennial spring and never failing autumn stand side by side, and towering snow-clad mountains forever look down upon eternal verdure."

The most glowing reports were, in fact, the most accurate. Few lovelier lands existed than that languid, dreamy California of the 1840s. Twenty years before, Spain, which had laid waste empires and decimated whole peoples in a merciless search for gold, had let California slip through its fingers—and with it, unknowing, a treasure in gold ore. Mexico, which obtained California along with its independence in 1821, had been almost as careless. There were no courts, no police, no postal facilities, no schools and there was almost no communication with Mexico City.

Soon after the Spanish yoke was slipped, even the discipline of religion had largely been thrown off. The landmarks of Spanish rule had been the Franciscan missions—entire villages complete with church, shops, schools and thriving farmlands, patiently tilled by the converted Indians, who had forsaken their native skills for the life of settled farmers. Typical was the beautiful mission of San Juan Bautista, which had boasted great orchards and vineyards and flower gardens, with its own olive presses and casks of brandy and wine. The church had a high redwood altar and was adorned by the best of Indian and Mexican art: beautiful paintings of the saints and gorgeous vestments woven in gold and silver.

But under loose Mexican rule the missions crumbled slowly into ruin, and

San Carlos de Borromeo was a serene and stately mission built by the Franciscan friars on Carmel Bay. In the compound formed by church, storehouses and workshops the Indians were taught farming, carpentry and weaving, the Spanish language and the Roman Catholic religion. Parts of the mission are still in existence serving as a parish church and museum.

the vast landholdings were seized and sold. A few courageous friars hung on; a few churches survived, with broken statues. The Indian converts were turned loose to shift for themselves, with near-tragic results.

When the Americans began arriving in the 1840s, they found a small and scattered population, at the apex of which were the aristocratic caballeros, whose easy-handed life, "half barbaric, half elegant," rivaled in romance and splendor the legendary Old South. Hospitality was the law of life, pleasure the primary goal. Ranchos, 40 miles square and sweeping from mountains to the sea, bloomed in a riot of color in the spring.

Yet much of the rich land was splashed with a different color—the gold of the feathery wild mustard. For the caballero did not farm; neither did he read nor engage in manual labor. The caballeros' clothes left the few Americans in California wide-eyed as these male peacocks with their curled hair, their gay silk vests, velvet breeches, their deerskin boots, embroidered jackets, and sombreros weighed down with gold and silver paraded their finery. The Californians spent their afternoons in siesta; they fought the cool of the evenings with serapes, large squares of colored cloth with slits for the head.

IT was a life too pleasant to last, too peaceful to remain undisturbed. The sleepy New Spain was doomed, first by the slowly encroaching pressure of the Americans, and second by the determination of James K. Polk. He had tried to buy California. If necessary, he would have gone to war for California. But he found it was not necessary.

Polk thought that California could be infiltrated as Texas had been—that is, by sending in enough Americans to stir up a ferment. To that end, in the spring of 1845, he dispatched Captain John Charles Frémont of the Army Topographers' Corps for a visit in the area. He had sent the right man to the right place. Frémont was already being called "the Pathfinder" for his Western exploits. His Western career would be a flamboyant blend of impulse and good public relations, and his much-vaunted "conquest" of California would have all the elements of comic opera.

In a land dedicated to chivalry and mannered living, Frémont knew well how to make an excellent impression. His mother had been a Whiting of Virginia, his father a French Royalist refugee. Unfortunately, although he was described as "the handsomest young man who ever walked the streets of Washington," he had been born out of wedlock. In a curious way this handicap

Fort Ross, with its redwood walls, blockhouses and Orthodox church, was a Russian settlement near San Francisco. Its inhabitants traded in sea otter skins and raised cattle there until 1841. Then, over a table of flowing wine, they sold the fort to settler John Sutter for a swindler's price. But that gave them little pleasure. One of their agents ran away with most of the money.

John C. Frémont, the explorer whose name is signed to some of the most galloping prose in American history, never really wrote much—writing gave him nosebleeds. It was his wife, Jessie Benton Frémont, who ghostwrote his reports in such sparkling language as: "Indians and buffalo were the poetry and life of the prairie, and our camp was full of their exhilaration."

both goaded him on and held him back. He had married Senator Benton's daughter Jessie, a vivacious, beautiful, dark-eyed young woman. These three, the senator, the soldier and the woman, all dedicated believers in Manifest Destiny, made a formidable team: Benton, "the Thunderer" who had cried out for years in Congress for the opening of the West; the dashing son-in-law who was now opening it; and the ambitious Jessie, who was already helping turn the reports of her husband's expeditions into treatises of literary distinction that were widely printed and eagerly read.

A first-rate leader, Frémont had started his Western career brilliantly. In his first two expeditions he had established the correct latitude and longitude of many frontier sites, suggested good locations for military posts and pioneer settlements and written glowing reports about the fertility of the lands between the Missouri River and the Rocky Mountains. But he had also had his share of troubles. On the second expedition, from St. Louis across Wyoming to Oregon, he insisted on dragging a cannon over the mountains, presumably to awe the Indians.

Frémont's superior, the chief topographer, Colonel John J. Abert, outraged at what he considered a preposterous act and fearful of provoking an international incident, recalled both the Pathfinder and his cannon. But Jessie, in St. Louis, did not forward Colonel Abert's letter, and the expedition pushed ahead. Frémont pulled the heavy cannon all the way from Missouri through snow and icy passes before abandoning it in the foothills of the Sierras. However, when he finally got through he had accomplished a spectacular feat. He had crossed the mountains in a season when the Indians said it could not be done. In the process he had found a route by which the United States Army could move into California should war occur. He returned to St. Louis, emaciated and exhausted.

After this came his errand for Polk. The 32-year-old Pathfinder traveled west under secret orders, reaching Sutter's Fort on the American River in December 1845. A month later, at Monterey, he sought official permission to purchase fresh supplies. His mission, he explained, was scientific, his men civilians, and his goal a geographic survey of the best route from the Atlantic to the Pacific Coast. He planned, he said, to explore the Colorado River. Despite his persuasiveness, the Mexican officials remained suspicious, although they did nothing to stop him.

But when he headed for the Southwest rather than toward Oregon or the Colorado, the officials began to worry. After all, Frémont was the son-in-law of Senator Benton, the notorious expansionist who was high in the councils of President Polk. At last the Mexicans lost patience and asked Frémont to leave California immediately. Instead, he defiantly built some fortifications, raised the American flag and announced that he would die fighting. But then he had second thoughts and withdrew toward Oregon—for a time.

F REMONT understood Polk's dilemma and he was prepared to solve it. The President wanted California, yet he could not send troops there as long as the country was not at war. And if he did not send troops he might lose the region. Polk had piously intimated that he would not take the fruit from another man's trees. But now the fruit was ripe and ready to fall, and John Charles Frémont was on the scene. His course seemed clear. If he took California *without* authorization from official Washington, no one could accuse Polk of stealing the province from Mexico. But Frémont would first have to resign from the federal service, so he could act as a private citizen, without implicating the American government.

In May, Frémont returned to California from Oregon and carefully submitted his resignation to Senator Benton in Washington, leaving to his father-in-law the decision on how to use this document. Then he incited American settlers to capture Sonoma, north of San Francisco, and to proclaim the "Bear Flag Republic." On June 14, they ran up a homemade flag emblazoned with "a particularly home-made semblance of a bear." On June 25, Frémont himself entered Sonoma at the head of his troops.

The Californians offered little resistance. Some blood was shed, but all of California north and west of San Francisco was in American hands by the time news arrived of the outbreak of the Mexican War. Soon the American flag was flying at all important points in California.

The real fight broke out between Commodore Robert F. Stockton and General Stephen Watts Kearny. Stockton had sailed to California with orders to seize the region and set up a government there. He took Santa Barbara and Los Angeles, named himself governor and officially proclaimed California to be part of the United States. Kearny, who had marched in from New Mexico with precisely the same orders, denied Stockton's authority.

Los Angeles, which had revolted in September, was retaken by Stockton and Kearny in a frontal charge. But it was Frémont, arriving two days later with about 400 newly recruited troops, who negotiated a treaty of surrender as "military commander," calmly going over the heads of both Commodore Stockton and General Kearny. Then Frémont chose to recognize Stockton as the officer in command. Incensed, Kearny invoked his over-all authority under fresh orders from Washington. Without letting Frémont join his regiment in Mexico as the President had suggested, or even letting him get the notes and scientific specimens he had collected, Kearny ordered the young rebel to accompany him to Fort Leavenworth, where the Pathfinder was put under arrest and sent to Washington.

F REMONT'S court-martial in the capital in the fall of 1847 was the most spectacular courtroom drama since the trial of Aaron Burr 40 years before. Everyone was there, and everyone's gaze was fixed on Benton, on Jessie and on Frémont, who seemed as calm "as if writing at his camp in the mountains." He was accused of doing precisely what he had been secretly ordered to do: instigating the Americans in California to revolt, leading an armed invasion on the pretext of conducting a scientific expedition, undertaking an unauthorized conquest and accepting an unauthorized surrender, and refusing to relinquish his command to an officer sent from the War Department.

The President now faced a new dilemma. To be sure, Frémont had disobeyed orders, but Polk felt it would not do to let him stand convicted of mutiny. When the court-martial found Frémont guilty, Polk quickly announced that in view of the accused's "meritorious and valuable services" he should be released from arrest and "resume his sword."

But Frémont had wanted complete exoneration, and not just from the President. Enraged at the court-martial ruling, he resigned from the army, while Senator Benton, "violent beyond . . . usual even for him," harangued the Senate for 13 days, opposing Kearny's promotion to major general. Kearny cared

Bold Commodore Robert F. Stockton, conqueror of southern California, loved adventure. In the Mediterranean he fought duels with British naval officers who derided the U.S. In Africa he was captured by tribesmen but saved his life with an eloquent speech and one gesture: "My hand," he explained, "held a pistol at full cock, pointed at the head of the chief."

Painted in pokeberry juice by William L. Todd, a nephew of Mrs. Abraham Lincoln, the California Bear Flag became for a time the American settlers' battle banner. "The b'ar," they explained, "always stands his ground." Mexicans sneered that the settlers' b'ar looked more like a hog to them.

Stumbling up out of their snow-buried cabins, survivors of the ill-fated Donner party greet rescuers in the Sierras. Once they reached the coast most of the Donner survivors prospered. Several of the girls were married within months of their rescue, and one member of the party opened a restaurant.

little; he was dying of fever contracted at Veracruz. Before he breathed his last he sent for Jessie, daughter and wife of the men who had once been his friends. Jessie refused to see him.

On January 24, 1848, shortly before the signing of the peace treaty with Mexico, gold was discovered at Sutter's Mill in California. The news traveled slowly at first, and even when it was received many Easterners pooh-poohed it as a publicity scheme. Then, suddenly, gold fever raged unchecked.

Almost overnight, sleepy, dreamy Latin California was transformed as huge throngs raced to the gold fields. The region's towns, farms, even ships and army posts were suddenly deserted, but the river valleys and the great silent mountains were filled with roaring camps. From all over the world, men came. Three quarters of them, however, were Americans. They arrived by ship—an eight-month journey around Cape Horn or a more perilous two months via the pestilential Isthmus of Panama—and they came by covered wagon, some 45,-000 crossing the Sierra Nevada in 1849 alone. Almost all the "forty-niners," as they were called, were young and some were well educated—the human foundation for California's future greatness. But few women came—only about 700 in 1849—and it was said that almost "any semblance of a woman could be . . . sure of a speedy marriage."

How much gold the miners took out is a question. One historian has estimated that in 1848 some $10 million was mined, an average of about $1,000 for each miner. This was a vast sum of money in those days—except in California, where miners were charged four dollars a pound for coffee, six dollars a pound for pork and $400 a barrel for flour.

The forty-niners transformed California. Picturesque in their standard attire of broad-brimmed hats, red shirts and boots, they were a bearded crew who swaggered about with revolvers and sometimes bowie knives, and paid for their drinks in pinches of gold dust. They swept away John Augustus Sutter's empire along the Sacramento, elbowing him out on the ground that his land claims were defective. They even surged onto Frémont's 43,000-acre Mariposa ranch, forcing him into a protracted lawsuit to establish his claim.

They flooded into San Francisco. In 1848 it had been a peaceful and industrious little town with a number of merchants and tradesmen. Suddenly it was a metropolis, roaring with vice and ridden with fever, its streets streams of mud, its hotels dirty and jammed—a city of tents and shanties. Hideous crimes went unpunished. In the early '50s, there were 1,000 murders with only one conviction, although several of the offenders were lynched.

The forty-niners studded the map with new places and place names: Dutch Flat, Kanaka Bar, Chinese Camp, Rattlesnake Diggings, Whiskey Slide, Flea Town, Brandy Gulch. New words and phrases, too, were working their way into the American language: ghost town, stake out, bonanza, clean up, cash in. The forty-niners started a massive, steady shift of population into California that was still going on a century later. Few of the forty-niners actually found fortunes. But they opened the Golden Gate.

THE miners were not the only settlers to come to California. After Frémont publicized his route through Wyoming's South Pass, a few covered wagons pushed through every year. It was still a grueling trip, and travelers worried about Indians, terrain and weather. Sometimes they did not worry enough.

In 1846 an especially large party of 87 headed west toward California, led by

George Donner, an elderly farmer from Illinois. They were well equipped with wagons and cash; the Donners alone had $10,000 in bank notes sewed into a quilt. Tamsen Donner, a Yankee schoolmarm, was taking notes for a book as the wagon wheels turned. She had also brought paints, schoolbooks and scientific apparatus for the young ladies' seminary she intended to start in California. The group was, in short, fitted for everything—except Western travel.

The Donner party lacked sufficient food and adequate clothing, and most of all they lacked experience. September came in with a stinging early snow, and it found the travelers high in the mountains, but on the wrong side of the Sierras. By now food supplies were dangerously low, the remaining wagons rickety, and the oxen and cows almost dead from hunger. The sky was heavy with snow clouds. The emigrants decided to winter near Truckee Lake. They built makeshift shelters. They tried to fish but the fish would not bite. They tried to hunt but the game was gone.

Seventeen—known as the "Forlorn Hope" group—started out to get help, moving through a white desolation of snow with a six-day supply of food, to be eaten at a rate of two mouthfuls a day. Two turned back; eight more of the Forlorn Hope party died on the way; the others cut up the dead bodies and ate them. After long weeks of agonizing effort, seven survivors of the Forlorn Hope group reached help.

The rescuers who arrived at Truckee Lake almost missed the Donner group, for they were in buried huts with no smoke to be seen. The figures who came whimpering up out of those holes in the snow were scarcely recognizable as human beings. In the two months since the Forlorn Hope party had left, their minds had been stripped down to insane chaos; some of the children were lying in their own filth. Jacob Donner's children were eating the half-roasted liver of their father. Another rescue group stumbled upon a kettle full of the pieces of the body of George Donner, dead but four days. Ironically, some frozen legs of oxen found in the snow had not been touched. Forty of the Donner party were gone. Forty-seven lived to see the Pacific.

THIS was the most ghastly single emigrant-train experience. But none of the early covered-wagon groups had an easy time of it. Perhaps because of the hardships they had undergone, these travelers were hard men and women when they reached California at last, mercilessly hard toward the easy-living natives they found. They had fought and struggled to get to California. Now they felt it belonged to them, and they were ruthless with the land claims of the Mexicans and even worse with the Indians.

With settlers flooding in, California was in need of a territorial government. But any discussion of this matter in Congress immediately raised the question of California's future statehood—and with it the question of slavery. The free and slave states were reaching a balance, and as it was clear that California would come in free, the South was opposing its admission—had been opposing it, in fact, since 1846.

The issue was boldly dramatized during the Mexican War. On August 8, 1846, Congressman David Wilmot of Pennsylvania—a plump, carelessly dressed man with untidy hair falling around a babyish face—rose in the House. He moved that pending territorial legislation be amended so that "neither slavery nor involuntary servitude shall ever exist" in any area acquired from Mexico. In the steaming hot summer, as candles and lamps smoldered while the Senate sat

Kit Carson (shown real above and in dime-novel glamor below) was a roving mountain man who could track wild animals and move unseen through Indian country. For years, he said, he "never slept under the roof of a house, or gazed upon the face of a white woman." He guided Frémont to California, and his place as a folk hero starts in the official reports of Frémont.

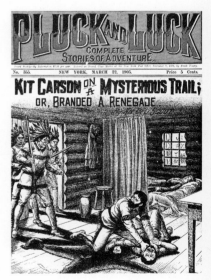

late and weary statesmen fanned themselves with newspapers, the tragic dilemma became clear. The South would balk if the Wilmot Proviso became law, and the antislavery forces were bent on making it law. The Wilmot Proviso was passed by the House, but failed in the Senate. Reintroduced in 1847, it met the same fate.

But no matter how often the Wilmot Proviso was voted down, it sprang up again and again. The new fact of American political life was that now, for the first time, slavery was seeking to expand where it had never been before—to California, New Mexico, Utah.

Lean, taut Senator Jefferson Davis of Mississippi, still on crutches from his Mexican War wound, denounced the "folly and fanaticism and pride and hate and corruption of the day" and urged the simple solution of secession. Let the South part in peace, he said, "let the flag of our Union be folded up entire . . . untorn by the unholy struggle of civil war."

At the White House, Polk was doggedly resolved that neither the empire he had won for the Union, nor the Union itself, should shatter on the rock of slavery. He watched anxiously as the 1848 presidential campaign got under way. General Taylor, a slaveholder, had been picked as the Whig candidate. But Lewis Cass of Michigan, the Democratic candidate, echoing Senator Stephen A. Douglas of Illinois, proposed that the slave question be left to the people in the new territories to decide for themselves. The slavery adherents at the Democratic Convention offered a proposal which would have extended slavery to California and New Mexico. In the Senate, John C. Calhoun supported a compromise that would have kept slavery out of Oregon, and would have delegated the decision in the other two territories to the United States Supreme Court.

In mid-August, after an all-night session, a final bill was passed—forbidding slavery in Oregon. An attempt to settle the issue in California and New Mexico by extending the Missouri Compromise line of 36° 30′ to the Pacific died in the course of business. Polk was still reviving this suggestion as late as November, fearful that if California were left unorganized it might fall prey to adventurers or even set itself up with Oregon as an independent republic and deprive the Union of the entire Pacific Coast.

By January of 1849, the President had changed his approach. California should be admitted immediately as a state, without even going through the territorial stage. Any territorial bill, Polk now realized, seemed sure to include the Wilmot Proviso; he would have to veto it, leaving California without a government. Moreover, under Calhoun's lead, the South was organizing to strike back at the North if the proviso passed. No one was sure what form its opposition would take, but in the House, Robert Toombs of Georgia was shouting: "I am for disunion."

The political parties were breaking apart over slavery as the presidential campaign reached its climax. A group called the "Conscience Whigs" had broken with the Whig party to take a strong stand against slavery. Antislavery Democrats had split off into a new Free-Soil party and nominated former President Van Buren to head their slate. This Free-Soil group allied with the Conscience Whigs, took as their slogan "Free Soil, Free Speech, Free Labor, and Free Men" and polled some 300,000 votes in the election. This was almost five times the antislavery vote of 1844, but the total was not enough to keep

CALIFORNIA

UNDER A NEW FLAG

California after the war had fewer than 15,000 white inhabitants, most of whom lived along the coastal road, El Camino Real, in tiny settlements like San Diego, Los Angeles and San Francisco, or at missions such as San Luis Obispo or Santa Barbara. Ten years later the population was 500,000, and most of it lived in gold-mining towns (brown dots), bearing such obviously American names as Scratch Gulch, Grizzly Flat and Fiddletown. Gold seekers poured in along the California, Old Spanish and Gila Trails—in 1864 alone 60,000 came—and others arrived by sea.

the Whigs from electing their military hero, the honest but politically inept Taylor. With Taylor as his successor Polk was more fearful than ever about the future of the Union.

January 1849 was a month of unrelieved gloom. To many, including Polk, it must have seemed the ebb of the nation itself. With the days of his presidency numbered, Polk knew that he, who had done more than anyone since Jefferson to enlarge the Union, might still see its dissolution.

Rarely had there been more talent in Congress to solve the problems that seemed insoluble: Mississippi's Jefferson Davis; William Seward of New York; the five-foot-two "Little Giant" from Illinois, Stephen A. Douglas, all dynamism and charm; the fiery Robert Barnwell Rhett of South Carolina; Toombs and Alexander Stephens of Georgia. And the old names, the familiar faces, were there too, all except the beloved Henry Clay, who had resigned from the Senate in 1842. But at 71 he had successfully stood for re-election. He would return to the Senate next fall.

Senator Sam Houston of Texas was there, clinging unwaveringly to the Union he had fought so hard to join. Thomas Hart Benton was aging, but the attractive mobile face retained its look of "the eagle and the lion." He could still fight with all his old ferocity, and his magnificent profanity and gigantic ego were unimpaired. Daniel Webster was still there; when he left it would be as if a mountain peak had dropped from the landscape. His powerful frame was as rocklike as ever, his craggy head as unforgettable; he was still, as Emerson described him, like a "great cannon loaded to the lips."

Calhoun was also there, 66 years old and hanging on to life by sheer force of will. In that January of 1849 he fainted on the Senate floor. He was burning with a relentless determination to reconcile impossibles, to save both the South and the Union. "*There*, indeed, is my only regret at going—the South, the poor South!" he said to Rhett.

Calhoun had a solution for the South which he knew entailed risks: he would stay in the Union, but counter threat with threat. He condemned the North's attacks on slavery, its refusal to return runaway slaves, to extend the Missouri Compromise to the Pacific, or to permit the slave South its fair share of the Mexican conquests. He implored Southerners to take a stand.

The South Carolinian's call for unified action dismayed Polk no less than the Wilmot Proviso had. Polk told Calhoun to his face that he "deemed it of the greatest importance that the agitation . . . of slavery . . . be arrested." Calhoun did not share Polk's belief that Northern agitation could be stilled by Southern silence; submission brought only further encroachments.

Oꜱ March 3, 1849, in accordance with the custom of retiring Presidents, Polk went to the Capitol. He had given up the idea of immediate statehood for California as impractical; now he sat in the Vice President's room near the Senate Chamber to await the last congressional acts of his presidency and to hope—against hope—that California would be granted territorial government free from the application of the Wilmot Proviso. If the proviso were tacked on, California would be voted down. Hour after hour dragged on; it was 1 o'clock, then 2, and "great confusion" prevailed in both houses. When the Senate finally defeated the provision creating a territorial government for California, Sam Houston grimly said: "I have seen order resolved from a mass of chaos, but I have never seen order resolved into chaos before."

MARRIED MUM ?

A lithograph pokes wry fun at a chief drawback in California—the scarcity of women. Any female who could give the answer below to the question above was assured a hearty welcome. But the New York "Tribune's" correspondent wrote dryly that "he who cannot make a bed, cook a beefsteak, or sew up his own rips and rents, is unfit to be a citizen of California."

NO SIR!

Of what did Polk think as he sat there at the end of his four busy presidential years? Perhaps of that Washington to which he had come first as a young congressman 24 years earlier. How it had changed—and yet how much more the whole nation had changed since the first President had taken his oath of office just 60 years ago. Only 8,000 people had lived in Washington even as late as 1800; there were 50,000 today. True, the city was still patchy and sprawling; mansions and government buildings jostled festering shanties; privies and pigsties dotted the back yards. But Pennsylvania Avenue had been paved. The Capitol was still topped by a temporary dome of wood, but at the other end of the avenue were the sweeping and beautiful White House grounds. Near the Capitol was the sight that sickened the abolitionists in Washington: a "sort of negro livery-stable," where droves of slaves were collected like cattle to be shipped to the Southern markets. But although slavery existed in the capital, of Washington's 13,000 Negroes, 10,000 were free.

And how the country had grown—perhaps the most amazing growth any nation had ever made in 60 years. No wonder the presidency had wearied Polk. He was still laboring within the limitations of the office as defined for George Washington, yet the press of business was incredibly heavier. The number of Americans had jumped from four million in 1790 to 23 million now. In 1849 alone, nearly 300,000 immigrants arrived.

Though 85 per cent of the American people still lived in rural areas, only a few nations were ahead of the United States as industrial centers. Whitney's cotton gin and his idea of interchangeable parts for industrial production, Fulton's steamboat, Morse's telegraph—these were commonplace now, but there was still wonder at the Yankee ingenuity which shipped New England ice insulated in sawdust to steaming India.

Polk's frontier Tennessee was now only a memory. Rail lines were spinning an ever more complicated network. Hundreds of river boats, gleaming with lights, were steaming up and down the Mississippi, the Ohio, the Missouri.

FOUR WHO FOUGHT TO SPREAD SLAVERY TO THE WEST

Senator Lewis Cass of Michigan opposed efforts to curb slavery in order to get Southern support for his 1848 Democratic presidential campaign. Lincoln compared him with an ox obeying his masters; Horace Greeley called him a "potbellied, mutton-headed cucumber." But later he supported the Union.

Fiery, frail Alexander Hamilton (Little Ellick) Stephens of Georgia never weighed more than a hundred pounds but his breast bore knife wounds won in a brawl. For want of a presidential candidate satisfactory to him in 1852, Stephens stubbornly voted for Daniel Webster, who was nine days dead.

Georgia's Robert Toombs, a cheerful fountain of eloquence and wit, was careless about consistency in some of his political stands. Challenged for having voted in Congress against policies that he later favored, he blandly replied: "Yes, it was a damn bad vote. But what are you going to do about it?"

South Carolina's aristocratic Robert Barnwell Rhett was born plain Robert Smith, but he changed his name to that of one of his more illustrious ancestors. He also acquired a certain touch of hauteur. When he lost an election his newspaper, the Charleston "Mercury," simply left the election unreported.

Cyrus McCormick had opened a plant for his reaper in Chicago in 1847 which soon would revolutionize prairie farming and transform Chicago into a great meat and grain center.

During these long hours of waiting as his Administration came to its end, Polk could look back on much that he could feel proud of. Because of him the continental United States now extended from sea to shining sea. It had nearly reached its final bounds. Only the Gadsden Purchase, Russian Alaska and Hawaii were yet lacking from the area that would comprise the future 50 states. He himself would never see the Rockies or the Great Plains, stretching from sunrise to sunset. He would never smell the sage or listen to the wind in the redwoods. Yet because of him, others would have these experiences. Because of him, all this was part of a greater Union.

Now, in the dim hour of dawn on March 4, 1849, Polk was roused from his cramped sleep by word from Congress. He read the bills presented for his signature. Congress had voted to extend the revenue laws to the territories—without the proviso. On Inauguration Day, Monday, March 5, 1849, Taylor did little to ease Polk's fears over the new President's lack of experience and ability. "A well-meaning old man," Polk confided to his diary, but "uneducated, exceedingly ignorant of public affairs, and . . . of very ordinary capacity." Taylor read his address "very badly as to . . . pronunciation," then blithely informed his predecessor that California and Oregon were really too far away to become members of the Union and that it would be better for them to set up an independent government.

But Polk had won; now he could truly lay his burden down. He had been the President of the whole country, of a united Union. And for all his doubts of Taylor, Polk knew him to be a man. The new Southern-born President would later warn that he would put down any move for secession as Jackson would have put it down—as a commanding general at the head of the troops. For a time at least, the Union would be preserved.

FOUR WHO BATTLED TO KEEP THE NEW LANDS FREE

New York's Senator William H. Seward was easygoing and gracious, but he personified in Southern eyes antislavery's "atrocious sentiment." Mississippi Congressman Lamar said Seward's "eye glowed and glared upon Southern Senators as though the fires of hell were burning in his heart."

Salmon Portland Chase, a future Chief Justice, practiced in Cincinnati, across the river from slave-holding Kentucky. He represented so many fugitive slaves in legal cases he was known as "the attorney general for runaway negroes." "Uncle Tom's Cabin" is based in part on his file of legal papers.

David Wilmot fell out with his fellow Democrats. He was maneuvered out of his seat in the House. He was accused of living in rum-stenched hotel rooms and of using "blasphemous profanity in trifling conversation." But he helped found the Republican party and returned to Washington as a U.S. Senator.

Martin Van Buren, running as a Free-Soiler, tipped the balance against Democratic candidate Lewis Cass in 1848 but he got only nine votes in all of Virginia. His friends cried "fraud." His enemies in Virginia agreed. They piously added: "And we're still looking for the man who voted nine times."

VISITING A MISSION, San Carlos de Borromeo, near the present-day Carmel, the members of a 1786 French expedition are welcomed by a line-up of Indians trained by the Franciscan Fathers.

Yankee El Dorado on Spanish soil

THERE was vast irony in the struggle over California in the middle 1800s. Originally the Spanish empire in the New World had been carved out by fierce seekers after treasure, while the Anglo-Saxon thrust westward had begun with settlers peaceably seeking land. But when the two forces came face to face in California the positions were reversed. The resident Californians—mostly indolent ranchers, peaceful Indians and missionaries *(above)*—were no match for the tough, practical Yankee traders and explorers who confronted them. And it was grubby but durable gold prospectors like the one at right who profited from the fabled El Dorado—the land of gold—which had long tormented the avaricious dreams of the conquistadors.

The gold rush of 1849 was the critical event of California history. The metal was discovered in 1848 on a vast tract owned by a Swiss settler named John Augustus Sutter, who had hoped to build an independent state called New Helvetia. The gold strike appalled him, for it threatened to upset his dreams. He wanted to keep word from getting to the outside world, but it was too big a story to keep quiet. Hints appeared in newspapers, travelers passed along rumors, a settlement storekeeper, bursting with the news, flashed a quinine bottle full of gold dust in the presence of a customer—and the secret was out. Soon New Helvetia was overrun by forty-niners from all over the world come to seek gold, and—as an unexpected dividend—found a brand-new state.

HUNTING GOLD, a bearded forty-niner—wearing the red flannel shirt that was virtually a miner's uniform—rides purposefully through the California forest in a portrait by artist Albertus Browere, who joined the gold rush to paint as well as pan for gold. From 1849 to 1853 the bulk of gold was found by miners like this, rudely equipped with pick, shovel, pan and bedroll.

The traditions of another era, doomed by time

SPANISH-SPEAKING California was a strange land in which the pride and hospitality of Old Castile were grafted upon a cow-country economy. Horsemanship was close to a religion. For the *vaqueros*, or cowboys, even a gory chore like butchering cattle was seen as a feat of skill and was performed from horseback with a special matador-like knife thrust. All the men congregated each year at big rodeos to drink, rope grizzlies *(below)* and make deals. Traffic in cattle got so big that Yankee traders called cowhides "California banknotes." The anachronistic ranchero life was doomed even before the first U.S. flag flew over the territory.

Roping a grizzly, early California "vaqueros" show off their skill in this painting by James Walker. The bears were hunted down primarily

because they attacked valuable cattle. But instead of being killed they were customarily captured, to be matched in fights with wild bulls.

The hard road to California

Trailside disasters, as in the picture above, were often the prelude to total tragedy. With hostile Indians about and food and water supplies low, the collapse of a family's oxen meant, at the least, the loss of its possessions. At worst it could mean horrible deaths for all of its members. But still the pioneers came.

144

Up to 1844 most covered wagons had been rolling westward over the plains and mountains to Oregon. Then some began turning south off the Oregon Trail at Soda Springs, Idaho, to cross the Nevada desert and the Sierras into California. After the discovery of gold, California was nearly everyone's goal.

The long route to the Pacific became known as the "trail of the moldering ox," for in their hurry the settlers took no time to bury oxen, horses and mules that died along the way, but left them to rot. Then they plodded onward, earnestly telling one another that "the mountains in Californey are solid gold."

Losers and winners in the great rush for gold

GOLD-RUSH VICTIM John Sutter (in the uniform of a California militia general) died poor in Washington trying to reclaim land overrun by miners when gold was discovered at his mill.

GOLD MINERS employ various methods including digging, rock clearing and panning of dirt for gold. In the right foreground a "cradle" sifts out ore by a washing process.

THE hordes of tenderfoot miners who rushed to Sutter's Mill were as unprepared for the life they found as picnickers caught in a hailstorm. Gold did not lie about for the picking but was deep in the earth or under icy mountain streams. Bushwhacking and claim jumping were such hazards that towns began administering vigilante justice. One crime-ridden camp reportedly changed its name from Old Dry Diggings to Hangtown. Living was hard in other ways. A bottle of "42 caliber whiskey" cost $100. Women were so scarce that crusty miners, identified by arm bands, danced ladies' parts at Sunday "jollifications." But one man found a five-pound nugget, another sifted out 30 pounds of gold dust in a month. Encouraged, the miners labored on.

SUCCESSFUL MINERS divide their week's take. One miner is using a delicately balanced scale as two partners watch. Others are getting drunk *(left)*, getting 40 winks *(rear)* and getting supper *(right)*.

The singular sights of a booming community

ONCE San Francisco had been just a sleepy Spanish-Mexican village. But when in 1849 some 800 ships put nearly 40,000 gold seekers ashore there, it became a boom town which has never been matched for astonishing growth and sheer, violent confusion. Gold-crazed crews abandoned small ships on the waterfront *(opposite)*, and shelter-hungry citizens moved in, extending the town out to the larger vessels by filling in the harbor with sand and debris. The city included a Little Chile, a French section called Keskedee (from *"Qu'est-ce qu'il dit?"*) and a band of Australian ex-convicts known as the "Sydney Ducks," who roamed the city robbing and killing. Prices were unimaginable: $10 for one tack, $150 for a sheet of paper. Only one homely item was reduced. A sudden influx of Chinese drove the cost of laundering a dozen shirts down to three dollars.

SHOREBOUND SHIPS, including an old sidewheeler, merge with a jungle of tents and ramshackle huts in an 1849 portrait of San Francisco by Spanish artist Augusto Ferran. Fire swept this inflammable hodgepodge six times in 18 months, leading to the construction of more solid wooden and brick buildings.

MIRED PEDESTRIANS make their hazardous way along a San Francisco street in this Francis Marryat caricature. People threw in boxes and barrels to act as stepping-stones. The quicksandlike mud was known to swallow up cats, drunks, even horses. "This street impassable," read a sign, "not even Jackassable."

MIXED DRINKERS at an ornate bar illustrate the city's polyglot population. From the left: cloaked Spanish-Mexican rancheros, four bearded Americans from the diggings, pigtailed Chinese and a top-hatted professional gambler. The man at right is giving his scalp a treatment with something stronger than bay rum.

A prospect of future glory

This panoramic view of burgeoning San Francisco was painted in 1850 by artist Ferran from behind present-day Telegraph and Russian Hills, which the sprawling city eventually encompassed. To the right the spreading curve of the hull-strewn waterfront, later known as the Barbary Coast, is backed by a

mushrooming tangle of tents and wooden houses. Beyond, the permanent fleet of 450 abandoned ships, rotting as their crews seek gold, swings idly at anchor in the great protected bay of which an early Spaniard had happily reported that the fleets "of all Europe could take shelter in it." Still farther out, the tiny island of Yerba Buena and the distant hills of modern Oakland lead the painter's eye to the glow of the sun setting over the Pacific—in historic witness that the centuries-old westward course of empire, the long dream of Spaniard and Yankee alike, was now firmly fixed upon the shore of the Western sea.

CHRONOLOGY — *A timetable of American and world events: 1829-1849*

WORLD EVENTS	EXPANSION and EXPLORATION	POLITICS	MILITARY and FOREIGN AFFAIRS	ECONOMICS and SCIENCE	THOUGHT and CULTURE
1829-46 Era of electoral reform in Great Britain; 1830 Independence of Greece and Belgium; 1830 France conquers Algiers; 1830-31 Insurrection in Poland; 1830-48 "July Monarchy" of Louis Philippe in France; 1831 Faraday discovers principle of electromagnetism; 1831 Victor Hugo's *Notre-Dame de Paris* published	1829 Formation of society for encouraging settlement of Oregon; 1830 Mexicans forbid further colonization of Texas; 1830 Fur trappers take first covered wagons to the Rockies; 1830-42 Indians east of the Mississippi forced to surrender their lands; 1831-32 Schoolcraft expedition discovers the source of the Mississippi	1828 Andrew Jackson elected President; 1828-34 "Labor parties" emerge in the United States; 1828-48 Broadened suffrage triples the popular vote; 1830 Webster-Hayne debate; 1830 Jackson and Calhoun trade Jefferson Day toasts; 1831 Anti-Masons hold first national nominating convention; 1831 Senator William Marcy coins "To the victor belong the spoils."; 1831-32 Jackson defies Supreme Court on Indian removals	1829 Jackson offers Mexico $5 million for Texas; 1830 Indian Removal Act; 1830 West Indies Trade, closed since 1826, reopened; 1831 French agree to pay damage claims for Napoleonic seizures	1830 New York, the largest American city since 1810, becomes commercial center of the New World; 1830 Peter Cooper's locomotive *Tom Thumb* makes first successful run; 1830 Census shows 12,866,020 inhabitants; 1831 Jerome Case founds thresher works, eventually world's largest; 1831 Discovery of chloroform	1829-78 William Cullen Bryant editor of New York *Evening Post*; 1830 Joseph Smith founds the Mormon Church; 1830 *Godey's Lady's Book* becomes the most popular journal of its type in the period; 1830-50 Height of the Shaker communal experiment; 1830-60 American sculpture influenced by Italian neoclassicism; 1831 De Tocqueville comes to America; 1831 Garrison founds *The Liberator*; 1831 Nat Turner slave insurrection in Virginia
1832 The Oregon Trail — 1832 British Reform Bill becomes law, widening suffrage; 1832 Mazzini founds "Young Italy" group, dedicated to Italian unification; 1834 Slavery abolished in the British colonies; 1834-39 Carlist Civil War in Spain; 1835 First German railway constructed; 1835-37 Great Trek of the Boers in South Africa	1832 Wyeth opens western part of the Oregon Trail; 1832-35 Bonneville leads expedition to Rockies; 1833 Chicago organized; 1833 Walker opens Yosemite Valley; 1833 Area now known as Iowa opened to settlement; 1834 First American missionaries in Oregon; 1834 First settlement in Idaho; 1835-40 Final period of Rocky Mountain fur trade	1832 South Carolina issues Ordinance of Nullification over tariff; 1832 Jackson vetoes rechartering of the United States Bank; 1832 Jackson re-elected President; 1833 Jackson answers South Carolina nullification with Force Bill; 1833 Clay and Calhoun formulate compromise tariff; 1833 Jackson removes government deposits from the U.S. Bank; 1834-37 First national labor organization in U.S., the National Trades Union; 1834-54 Rise and fall of the Whig Party	1832 Black Hawk War; 1832 Rebirth of the United States Cavalry; 1832 Congress creates Bureau of Indian Affairs in War Department; 1832 Skirmishes between Mexicans and Texans; 1835-36 Texas War of Independence; 1835-42 Second Seminole War	1832-56 Wabash and Erie Canal, longest in the U.S., built; 1834 McCormick takes out first patent on reaper; 1834 Benton coinage act fixes gold-silver ratio at 16-1; 1834 First use of federal troops in labor dispute, in Maryland; 1834-39 Davenport invents electric motor; 1835 First gas lighting in an American hotel, in Boston; 1835 Colt patents revolver	1832 Boston Academy of Music opened; 1832 Clay coins term "self-made" man; 1833 Formation of the American Anti-Slavery Society; 1833 Oberlin College founded, first coeducational college; 1833 Disestablishment of the Congregational Church in Massachusetts; 1833 New York *Sun* first successful penny paper; 1834 N. Currier founds business later called Currier & Ives; 1834 New York's *Staats-Zeitung* claims largest German-language circulation; 1834 Anti-Catholics burn Ursuline convent in Massachusetts
1836 Remember the Alamo! — 1836 Louis Napoleon fails in coup attempt to seize power in France and is exiled; 1836 Charles Dickens' first successful book, *The Pickwick Papers*, published; 1836 First trains from London to Greenwich; 1836-48 Chartist Movement in Great Britain attempts to achieve social equality and universal suffrage; 1837-38 Papineau Rebellion in Canada; 1837-1901 Reign of Victoria in Britain	1836 Arkansas statehood; 1836 Organization of the Wisconsin Territory; 1837 Congress receives first detailed account of Oregon settlements; 1837 Michigan statehood; 1837 Minnesota Territory opened to settlement; 1838 Iowa Territory organized	1835 New York radicals form Locofoco faction of Democratic party; 1835 Taney succeeds Marshall as Chief Justice; 1836 Anti-Masons coalesce with Whigs; 1836 Martin Van Buren elected President; 1836-44 Gag rule on antislavery petitions brings abolitionism into politics; 1837 Vice-presidential election forced into Senate; Richard M. Johnson wins; 1837 Censure resolution of Jackson expunged	1836 Battles of the Alamo and San Jacinto; 1837 Texans petition for annexation by U.S. but are rebuffed; 1837 U.S. recognition of Texas; 1837-42 Border friction with Canada; 1838-39 Aroostook "War" over Maine boundary; 1839-40 Texas	1836 Dinosaur tracks found in Connecticut Valley; 1836 Friction match receives American patent; 1836 Specie Circular requires hard-money payment in land sales; 1836 Connecticut passes first incorporation law in U.S.; 1837 John Deere makes steel plow; 1837 Morse and Cooke invent telegraph; 1837-43 Banking panic throws country into depression; 1839 First comprehensive work on pathology by Samuel D. Gross; 1839 First congressional appropriation of...	1836 First editions of *The McGuffey Readers*; 1836 Group of Boston and Concord intellectuals form Transcendental Club; 1836 Formation of the American Temperance Union; 1837 Mount Holyoke first permanent women's college; 1837 Emerson address on "The American Scholar"; 1837-48 Elijah Lovejoy, abolitionist editor, murdered; 1837-48 Horace Mann on Massachusetts Board of Education; 1838 Garrison organizes New England Non-Resistance Society; 1838 James Fenimore Cooper's *The American Democrat* published; 1839

Top section (1840–1844)

expedition in the South Pacific explores part of Antarctica
1840 "Permanent Indian Frontier" declared along 95th meridian
1840-46 Jesuit missionaries in Oregon
1841 Congress passes Pre-Emption Act to aid squatters
1841 Overland migration to California begins
1842 Frémont explores the Wind River range
1842-43 Large-scale immigration to Oregon
1843 Oregon settlers adopt provisional constitution
1843-44 Frémont in California
1844 George Henry Evans begins homestead agitation

1840 William Henry Harrison elected President
1840 Federal employees get 10-hour day
1841 Harrison first President to die in office, succeeded by John Tyler
1841 *Amistad* case frees Negroes who mutinied aboard a slave ship
1841-42 Tyler wars with Clay over policy and is read out of Whig party
1842 Dorr Rebellion in Rhode Island
1842 *Prigg vs. Pennsylvania* denies state obligation to enforce Fugitive Slave Laws
1842 Clay resigns Senate seat to run for President
1842 *Commonwealth vs. Hunt* repudiates common-law theory of labor conspiracy
1844 Whigs and Nativists elect anti-Catholic mayor in New York
1844 Clay-Van Buren letters on Texas
1844 James K. Polk elected President

1842 Webster-Ashburton Treaty settles northeastern boundary
1842 U.S. Arsenal makes last flintlock
1842 U.S. recognizes independence of Hawaii
1843 Santa Anna declares that U.S. annexation of Texas would mean war
1844 First commercial treaty with China

1840 Astronomy observatory erected at Harvard
1840 First production of pig iron using anthracite coal
1840 onward Westward shift of livestock production
1840 onward Tobacco industry revived in the South
1841 Building of U.S.S. *Princeton* begins, first propeller-driven man-of-war
1841 Mercantile Agency, first credit-rating organization, established
1842 Railroad completed from Albany to Buffalo
1842 First commercial artificial fertilizer developed
1843-60 Age of the Clipper Ship
1844 Asa Whitney projects a transcontinental railroad
1844 Goodyear perfects and patents vulcanization of rubber
1844 onward Iron rails replace wood on railroads

1840 *Two Years Before the Mast*, by Richard H. Dana, published
1840 onward Reform Judaism develops
1840-44 *The Dial*, Transcendentalist literary review
1841 Horace Greeley founds the New York *Tribune*
1841 Cooper's *The Deerslayer* published
1841-47 Transcendentalists sponsor Brook Farm
1842 American Protestant Association consolidates anti-Catholic groups
1842 Edwin P. Christy forms original minstrel troupe
1843 Dorothea Dix attacks existing treatment of the insane
1843 Millerites prepare for the end of the world
1843-44 Baptists and Methodists divide sectionally over slavery
1843-55 Fourierist Phalanx practices utopian socialism in New Jersey
1844 Joseph Smith lynched; Brigham Young succeeds to Mormon leadership
1844 Anti-Catholic riots in Philadelphia

1845 Manifest Destiny

League formed in Britain to end tariff on grain
1839 British seize Hong Kong
1839 Louis Daguerre's photographic process is revealed to the world
1839-42 First Opium War in China
1840 Upper and Lower Canada united
1841 Dardanelles and Bosporus closed to warships by European agreement in times of peace
1842 Riots in British manufacturing districts
1843 First performance of Wagner's opera, *The Flying Dutchman*
1844 Factory Act regulates hours for women and children in British industry

1845 Potato blight strikes Ireland, leading to great famine
1846 Repeal of Corn Laws
1846-78 Pius IX, Pope
1847 Liberia proclaimed independent republic
1847 *Jane Eyre*, by Charlotte Brontë, published
1848 Insurrections throughout Europe force Metternich into retirement
1848 Marx and Engels issue *Communist Manifesto*
1848 France becomes a republic, elects Louis Napoleon president
1848 Serfdom abolished in Austria
1848 Slavery abolished in French colonies
1849 Garibaldi marches into Rome
1849 Hungarian independence movement crushed, Kossuth exiled
1849 Britain encourages world trade by repealing 200-year-old Navigation Laws
1849-61 Macaulay writes *History of England*

1845 Florida and Texas statehood
1845 John L. O'Sullivan coins term "Manifest Destiny"
1846 Iowa statehood
1846-47 Donner party, snowbound in the Sierras, reduced to cannibalism
1847 The Mormons reach Utah
1847 Cayuse Indians massacre the Whitman group in Oregon
1848 First Chinese arrive in California
1848 Wisconsin statehood
1848 United States in possession of almost all the present Southwest
1848 Oregon organized as a free territory
1848 Discovery of gold in California touches off "Gold Rush"
1849 Mormons proclaim State of Deseret

1845 Native American Party holds first national convention
1845 Democratic party split in New York
1846 Wilmot Proviso introduced to ban slavery in newly acquired territory
1846-57 Dred Scott sues unsuccessfully for his freedom
1848 Martin Van Buren leaves the Democrats and joins new Free Soil party
1848 Zachary Taylor elected President
1849 Southern congressmen caucus to oppose antislavery legislation
1849 Department of the Interior established
1849 California constitution prohibits slavery

1845 Annexation of Texas by joint resolution
1845 Polk expands the Monroe Doctrine
1845 Thomas Larkin, U.S. consul in Monterey, appointed confidential agent to detach California from Mexico
1845 U.S. Naval Academy opened
1846 Settlement of Oregon Boundary
1846 Frémont aids Bear Flag revolt in California
1846-48 War with Mexico
1847 Battles of Monterrey, Buena Vista, Churubusco and Chapultepec
1847 Doniphan march to Chihuahua
1848 Treaty of Guadalupe Hidalgo ends Mexican War

1845 New York boasts of 21 millionaires
1846 Pennsylvania Railroad chartered
1846 Elias Howe invents sewing machine
1846 Founding of the Smithsonian Institution by Act of Congress
1846 Louis Agassiz comes to America to teach zoology and geology
1846 Walker Tariff lowers duties
1846 Anesthesia, first applied to surgery in 1842, comes into general use
1847 McCormick and others open reaper factory in Chicago
1847 Richard Hoe develops rotary printing press
1847 American Medical Association founded
1847 First U.S. adhesive postage stamp issue authorized by Congress
1848 American Association for the Advancement of Science founded
1849 Dr. Elizabeth Blackwell becomes first female doctor
1849 Invention of the safety pin

1845 Poe publishes poem "The Raven"
1845 *Leonora*, by William H. Fry, first grand opera composed by a native American
1845-47 Thoreau lives at Walden Pond
1846 Maine prohibits sale of liquor
1846-47 Melville writes *Typee* and *Omoo*
1847 Henry Wadsworth Longfellow completes "Evangeline"
1848 "Oh, Susannah" by Stephen Foster copyrighted
1848 Oneida Community established by John H. Noyes
1848 First Women's Rights Convention at Seneca Falls, New York
1849 Edwin Booth makes acting debut in Boston

FOR FURTHER READING

*These books were selected for their interest and authority in the preparation
of this volume, and for their usefulness to readers seeking additional information on specific points.
An asterisk (*) marks works available in both hard-cover and paperback editions.*

GENERAL READING

Agar, Herbert, *The People's Choice*. Houghton Mifflin, 1933.

Bailey, Thomas A., *A Diplomatic History of the American People*. Appleton-Century-Crofts, 1958.

Carman, Harry J., Harold C. Syrett and Bernard W. Wishy, *A History of the American People* (Vol. I). Alfred A. Knopf, 1960.

Current, Richard N., *Daniel Webster and the Rise of National Conservatism*. Little, Brown, 1955.

Fuess, Claude M., *Daniel Webster* (2 vols.). Little, Brown, 1930.

Hofstadter, Richard, William Miller and Daniel Aaron, *The American Republic* (Vol. I). Prentice-Hall, 1959.

McMaster, John Bach, *A History of the People of the United States, from the Revolution to the Civil War* (8 vols.). Appleton-Century, 1883-1913.

Morison, Samuel Eliot, and Henry Steele Commager, *The Growth of the American Republic* (Vol. I). Oxford University Press, 1962.

*Parrington, Vernon L., *Main Currents in American Thought*. Harcourt, Brace & World, 1939.

Van Deusen, Glyndon G., *The Jacksonian Era: 1828-1848*. Harper & Row, 1959. *The Life of Henry Clay*. Little, Brown, 1937. *Thurlow Weed, Wizard of the Lobby*. Little, Brown, 1947.

THE JACKSON ERA (CHAPTERS 1, 2)

Bemis, Samuel Flagg, *John Quincy Adams and the Union*. Alfred A. Knopf, 1956.

Bowers, Claude G., *The Party Battles of the Jackson Period*. Houghton Mifflin, 1922.

*Coit, Margaret L., *John C. Calhoun*. Houghton Mifflin, 1950.

Coyle, David C., *Ordeal of the Presidency*. Public Affairs Press, 1960.

Cresson, William P., *James Monroe*. University of North Carolina Press, 1946.

Eaton, Clement, *The Growth of Southern Civilization, 1790-1860*. Harper & Row, 1961. *The History of the Old South*. Macmillan, 1949.

Foreman, Grant, *Indian Removal: The Emigration of the Five Civilized Tribes of Indians*. University of Oklahoma Press, 1956.

Hammond, Bray, *Banks and Politics in America from the Revolution to the Civil War*. Princeton University Press, 1957.

Hodge, Frederick W. (ed.), *Handbook of American Indians North of Mexico* (Vol. II). Pageant, 1959.

*James, Marquis, *Andrew Jackson, The Border Captain*. Bobbs-Merrill, 1933. *Andrew Jackson, Portrait of a President*. Bobbs-Merrill, 1937.

*Mayer, Jacob P., *Alexis de Tocqueville: A Biographical Study in Political Science*. Peter Smith, 1960.

Newhall, Beaumont, *The Daguerreotype in America*. Duell, Sloan and Pearce, 1961.

Paxson, Frederic L., *History of the American Frontier, 1763-1893*. Houghton Mifflin, 1924.

*Peterson, Merrill D., *The Jefferson Image in the American Mind*. Oxford University Press, 1960.

Pollack, Peter, *The Picture History of Photography*. Harry N. Abrams, 1958.

*Schlesinger, Arthur M., Jr., *The Age of Jackson*. Little, Brown, 1945.

Smith, Margaret, *The First Forty Years of Washington Society* (ed. by Gaillard Hunt). Scribner's, 1906.

Sydnor, Charles, *The Development of Southern Sectionalism, 1819-1848*. Louisiana State University Press, 1948.

Tebbel, John W., and Keith W. Jennison, *The American Indian Wars*. Harper & Row, 1960.

*Tocqueville, Alexis de, *Democracy in America* (ed. by Henry Steele Commager, tr. by Henry Reeve). Oxford University Press, 1947.

Wiltse, Charles M., *John C. Calhoun* (Vol. II). Bobbs-Merrill, 1949.

THE IDEALISTIC EXPERIMENTS (CHAPTER 3)

*Brooks, Van Wyck, *The Flowering of New England, 1815-1865*. Dutton, 1937.

Dulles, Foster Rhea, *Labor in America: A History*. Thomas Y. Crowell, 1960.

Hutchison, William R., *The Transcendentalist Ministers*. Yale University Press, 1959.

*Melcher, Marguerite F., *The Shaker Adventure*. Princeton University Press, 1941.

Newcomer, Mabel, *A Century of Higher Education for American Women*. Harper & Row, 1959.

Nordhoff, Charles, *The Communistic Societies of the U.S.* Hillary House, 1960.

Tharp, Louise Hall, *The Peabody Sisters of Salem*. Little, Brown, 1950.

*Thoreau, Henry David, *Walden*. Thomas Y. Crowell, 1961.

*Tyler, Alice F., *Freedom's Ferment*. University of Minnesota Press, 1944.

EXPANSION TO THE WEST (CHAPTERS 4, 5, 6)

Agar, Herbert, *Pursuit of Happiness*. Houghton Mifflin, 1938.

Atherton, Gertrude F., *Golden Gate Country*. Duell, Sloan and Pearce, 1945.

Bakeless, John, *Daniel Boone*. Morrow, 1939.

Bill, Alfred Hoyt, *Rehearsal for Conflict: The War with Mexico, 1846-1848*. Alfred A. Knopf, 1947.

Billington, Ray A., *The Far Western Frontier: 1830-1860*. Harper & Row, 1956.

Caughey, John W., *California*. Prentice-Hall, 1953.

Chambers, William N., *Old Bullion Benton, Senator from the New West: Thomas Hart Benton*. Little, Brown, 1956.

Day, Donald, *Big Country: Texas*. Duell, Sloan and Pearce, 1947.

DeVoto, Bernard, *Across the Wide Missouri*. Houghton Mifflin, 1947. *The Year of Decision: 1846*. Houghton Mifflin, 1950.

Elliott, Charles Winslow, *Winfield Scott, the Soldier and the Man*. Macmillan, 1937.

Eyre, Alice, *The Famous Fremonts and Their America*. Christopher Publishing House, 1961.

Freeman, Douglas Southall, *R. E. Lee: A Biography* (Vol. I). Scribner's, 1934.

Friend, Llerena, *Sam Houston: The Great Designer*. University of Texas Press, 1954.

Graebner, Norman A., *Empire on the Pacific*. Ronald Press, 1955.

Hamilton, Holman, *Zachary Taylor* (2 vols.). Bobbs-Merrill, 1941-1951.

Henry, Robert S., *The Story of the Mexican War*. Frederick Ungar, 1961.

Houston, Sam, *Autobiography* (ed. by Donald Day and Harry Herbert Ullom). University of Oklahoma Press, 1954.

Jacobs, Melvin C., *Winning Oregon*. Caxton Printers, Ltd., 1938.

*James, Marquis, *The Raven: A Biography of Sam Houston*. Bobbs-Merrill, 1953.

Jeffries, Ona G., *In and Out of the White House*. Wilfred Funk, 1960.

Lewis, Lloyd, *Captain Sam Grant*. Little, Brown, 1950.

McCoy, Charles A., *Polk and the Presidency*. University of Texas Press, 1960.

Montgomery, Richard G., *The White-Headed Eagle*. Macmillan, 1938.

Morrel, Martha M., *Young Hickory: The Life and Times of President James K. Polk*. Dutton, 1949.

Nevins, Allan, *Frémont: Pathmarker of the West* (Vol. I). Frederick Ungar, 1962.

Polk, James K., *Diary of a President, 1845-1849* (ed. by Allan Nevins). Longmans, Green, 1952.

Rich, E. E., *Hudson's Bay Company, 1670-1870* (Vol. III). Macmillan, 1961.

*Singletary, Otis A., *The Mexican War*. University of Chicago Press, 1960.

Smith, Justin H., *The Annexation of Texas*. Barnes & Noble, 1941. *The War with Mexico* (2 vols.). Macmillan, 1919.

Stephenson, Nathaniel W., *Texas and the Mexican War*. Yale University Press, 1921.

*Stewart, George R., *Donner Pass*. California Historical Society, 1960.

Thomas, Benjamin P., *Abraham Lincoln*. Alfred A. Knopf, 1952.

Wellman, Paul I., *Gold in California*. Houghton Mifflin, 1958.

Wiltse, Charles M., *John C. Calhoun* (Vol. III). Bobbs-Merrill, 1951.

Zollinger, James P., *Sutter, the Man and His Empire*. Oxford University Press, 1939.

ACKNOWLEDGMENTS

The editors of this book are particularly indebted to the following persons and institutions for their assistance in the preparation of this volume: Eric L. McKitrick, Associate Professor, Columbia University, New York City; Archibald DeWeese, New York Public Library; Elizabeth Clare and William Davidson, Knoedler Galleries, New York City; Dorothea Shipley, Old Print Shop, Inc., New York City; Milton Kaplan, Library of Congress, Washington, D.C.; Beaumont Newhall and Robert Dodie, Eastman House, Rochester, New York; Mary C. Black, Abby Aldrich Rockefeller Folk Art Collection, Williamsburg, Virginia; Mary Frances Rhymer, Chicago Historical Society; Joseph A. Baird Jr., California Historical Society, San Francisco; Carl S. Dentzel and Ella Robinson, Southwest Museum, Los Angeles; and Judy Higgins.

The author, for her part, wishes to thank three of her colleagues at Fairleigh Dickinson University—Professor and Mrs. John Dollar and Dr. Kenneth MacKenzie—for their many valuable criticisms and suggestions in the preparation of the manuscript of *The Sweep Westward;* she also extends her appreciation for the assistance given her by Clifford Beebee, Stephen F. Cohen, Albert E. Elwell, Alice Grundman, Kathleen Hoagland, Louise Kirscher, Olga Podtiaguine, Henry Poleti and her parents, Mr. and Mrs. Archa W. Coit.

PICTURE CREDITS

The sources for the illustrations in this book are shown below. Credits for pictures from left to right are separated by semicolons, top to bottom by dashes. Sources have been abbreviated as follows: Bettmann— The Bettmann Archive; Brown—Brown Brothers; Culver—Culver Pictures; LC—Library of Congress; N-YHS—The New-York Historical Society, N.Y.C.; NYPL—The New York Public Library; N.Y. State Hist. Assn.—New York State Historical Association, Cooperstown.

Cover—Herbert Orth, The Knoedler Galleries, New York.

End papers drawn by Thomas Vroman.

CHAPTER 1: 6—*Andrew Jackson* by Thomas Sully, National Gallery of Art, Washington, D.C., Mellon Collection. 8, 9—Kennedy Galleries, New York; courtesy The Historical Society of Pennsylvania. 10, 11—NYPL; courtesy The Historical Society of Pennsylvania. 12—Bettmann. 13, 15, 16—Culver. 18, 19—Culver except top left Bettmann. 20, 21—The Edward W. C. Arnold Collection, lent by The Metropolitan Museum of Art, photograph courtesy Museum of The City of New York; F. V. Raymond, courtesy Cincinnati Art Museum. 22, 23—*Dennison Hill, Southbridge, Massachusetts* (artist unknown), National Gallery of Art, Washington, D.C. From the collection of Edgar William and Bernice Chrysler Garbisch—Jahn & Ollier Engraving Co., Abby Aldrich Rockefeller Folk Art Collection, Williamsburg, Virginia; Jahn & Ollier Engraving Co., *Flax Scutching Bee*, Linton Park, National Gallery of Art, Washington, D.C. From the collection of American Primitive Paintings given by Edgar William and Bernice Chrysler Garbisch. 24, 25—From the collection of Harry T. Peters, Jr., courtesy American Heritage Publishing Co., Inc. 26, 27—Left: *Godey's Lady's Book*, courtesy American Heritage Publishing Co., Inc.—The J. Clarence Davies Collection, Museum of The City of New York—courtesy Museum of The City of New York; center left: courtesy American Antiquarian Society, Worcester, Mass.—The Edward W. C. Arnold Collection, lent by The Metropolitan Museum of Art, photograph courtesy Museum of The City of New York; center bottom: courtesy Museum of The City of New York; center right: NYPL—The Edward W. C. Arnold Collection, lent by The Metropolitan Museum of Art, photograph courtesy Museum of The City of New York—courtesy Museum of The City of New York; right: Bettmann—courtesy Museum of The City of New York. 28, 29—Left: Courtesy LC—Eric Schaal, courtesy The Metropolitan Museum of Art, purchase, Rogers Fund, 1943; right: Eric Schaal, collection Mr. and Mrs. Screven Lorillard, Far Hills, N.J. 30, 31—Eric Schaal, NYPL—Herbert Orth, courtesy Smithsonian Institution. 32, 33—Collection of Edgar William and Bernice Chrysler Garbisch.

CHAPTER 2: 34—Fernand Bourges, courtesy of Fogg Art Museum, Harvard University Collection. 36, 37—Brown; Bettmann; courtesy The Historical Society of Pennsylvania. 38, 39—Courtesy American Antiquarian Society, Worcester, Mass.—Gimbels Coin Department; Sy Seidman; Bettmann. 40, 41—Bettmann—courtesy American Antiquarian Society, Worcester, Mass. 42, 43—Bettmann; Brown. 44—Ayer collection, Newberry Library, Chicago. 45—Courtesy Smithsonian Institution, Bureau of American Ethnology. 46, 47—N.Y. State Hist. Assn.; Bettmann. 48, 49—Courtesy Fanueil Hall; courtesy American Heritage Publishing Co., Inc. 50, 51—In the Collection of The Corcoran Gallery of Art. 52, 53—N.Y. State Hist. Assn. except top left courtesy American Antiquarian Society, Worcester, Mass. 54, 55—Harry Shaw Newman, The Old Print Shop, Inc., N.Y.C.—courtesy LC. 56, 57—Harry Shaw Newman, The Old Print Shop, Inc., N.Y.C.

CHAPTER 3: 58—Courtesy of The White House. 60, 61—Bettmann (2); Culver (2); Bettmann; Culver; Mercantile Library; Bettmann. 62, 63—Bettmann. 64—Mercantile Library. 66, 67—Bettmann except bottom right Herbert Orth, Massachusetts Historical Society. 68, 69—The George Eastman House Collection; by permission of Brown University Library, Providence, Rhode Island. 70—The Metropolitan Museum of Art, gift of I. N. Phelps Stokes, Edward S. Hawes, Alice Mary Hawes, Marion Augusta Hawes, 1937. 71—The Metropolitan Museum of Art, gift of I.N. Phelps Stokes, Edward S. Hawes, Alice Mary Hawes, Marion Augusta Hawes, 1937; copy by R. Peter Petersen, Museum of Modern Art, N.Y.C., gift of A. Conger Goodyear; The George Eastman House Collection—Culver—N-YHS; The Metropolitan Museum of Art, gift of I. N. Phelps Stokes, Edward S. Hawes, Alice Mary Hawes, Marion Augusta Hawes, 1937; The George Eastman House Collection. 72—The George Eastman House Collection, gift of A. Conger Goodyear; Chicago Historical Society—The Metropolitan Museum of Art, gift of I. N. Phelps Stokes, Edward S. Hawes, Alice Mary Hawes, Marion Augusta Hawes, 1937; Chicago Historical Society. 73—The Metropolitan Museum of Art, gift of I.N. Phelps Stokes, Edward S. Hawes, Alice Mary Hawes, Marion Augusta Hawes, 1937. 74, 75—Courtesy of the Public Library of Cincinnati and Hamilton County. 76, 77—Courtesy Mrs. Joseph Carson and American Heritage Publishing Co., Inc.; The George Eastman House Collection—courtesy American Antiquarian Society, Worcester, Mass.; from a daguerreotype by Southworth & Hawes, Holman's Print Shop Inc., Boston. 78, 79—Courtesy Zelda P. Mackay, San Francisco, Calif.; The George Eastman House Collection.

CHAPTER 4: 80—Courtesy of The White House. 82, 83—Bettmann; Culver. 84, 85—Texas Heritage Foundation, Inc., A. Garland Adair, Ex. Dir.; The Texas Bankers Association. 86, 87—Courtesy LC; N.Y. State Hist. Assn. 88, 89—Culver. 91—Culver—N.Y. State Hist. Assn. 92, 93—NYPL; courtesy San Jacinto Museum of History and American Heritage Publishing Co., Inc. 94, 95—By courtesy of the Daughters of the Republic of Texas Library at the Alamo, reproduction of any or all pictures by permission only except top left *Stephen F. Austin*, by H. McArdle, De Venny-Wood Studio, permission to reproduce given by Texas House of Representatives. 96, 97—Courtesy Mrs. J. B. Arthur, Mrs. Melba Warner, San Antonio, Texas and American Heritage Publishing Co., Inc., painting on display at the Witte Memorial Museum, San Antonio, Texas, Dr. Wm. Burns, Director. 98, 99—Messina Studios, collection of the DeGolyer Foundation, Dallas, Texas; Texas State Library, Austin, courtesy American Heritage Publishing Co., Inc.

CHAPTER 5: 100—Chicago Historical Society. 102, 103—Bettmann; NYPL. 105, 106, 107—Bettmann. 108, 109—NYPL (2); Bettmann. 110, 111—Bettmann; Culver. 112, 113—Courtesy LC; Culver. 114 through 127—Herbert Orth.

CHAPTER 6: 128—The Corcoran Gallery of Art. 130, 131—Peabody Museum, Harvard University; courtesy LC. 132, 133—Courtesy LC; Bettmann. 134—Bettmann. 135—NYPL; courtesy Edward T. Le Blanc. 137—Henry H. Baskerville, courtesy Robert B. Honeyman, Jr. 138, 139—Culver; Bettmann (2); collection South Carolina Historical Society; Bettmann (2); NYPL; Culver. 140, 141—NYPL; Herbert Orth, The Knoedler Galleries, New York. 142, 143—Henry H. Baskerville, courtesy California Historical Society, gift of Charles Ernest von Geldern—Henry H. Baskerville, courtesy California Historical Society, gift of Mr. and Mrs. Reginald Walker. 144, 145—Henry H. Baskerville, Stanford University Museum. 146, 147—Left: Henry H. Baskerville, courtesy of the State of California; right: Henry H. Baskerville, Stanford University Museum—Herbert Orth, The Knoedler Galleries, New York. 148—J. R. Eyerman, courtesy Robert B. Honeyman, Jr. 149—Herbert Orth, N-YHS. 150, 151—J. R. Eyerman, courtesy Robert B. Honeyman Jr.

Back cover—Bettmann.

INDEX

*This symbol in front of a page number indicates a photograph or painting of the subject mentioned.

Production Staff for Time Incorporated

Arthur R. Murphy Jr. (Vice President and Director of Production)
Robert E. Foy, James P. Menton and Caroline Ferri
Text photocomposed under the direction of Albert J. Dunn and Arthur J. Dunn

x

Printed by The Safran Printing Company, Detroit, Michigan
Bound by Rand McNally & Company, Hammond, Indiana
Paper by The Mead Corporation, Dayton, Ohio